PERENNIALS

An Adrian Bloom Gardening Guide

JARROLD COLOUR PUBLICATIONS · NORWICH

PREFACE

In recent years there has been a surge in the popularity of Perennials both in Britain, Europe and North America. There are of course good reasons why this should be so, for in few families of plants is there such diversity or adaptability, such ranges of colour and form.

One can find Perennial plants to suit almost any site or situation. There are plants for woodland, including many native North American, European and Japanese native plants; plants for ground cover; for moisture or waterside; Perennials for associating with shrubs – and of course, an amazing variety which can be used in borders or beds on their own.

After the Second World War, Perennials seemed to lose some of their popularity in Britain. This was partly due to the disappearance of many larger gardens with their traditional 'herbaceous border'. Also, many kinds were too tall to adapt to the smaller garden and others created a maintenance problem. I would not think too many people who know Perennials would disagree when I state that my father, Alan Bloom, was probably more instrumental in popularising Hardy Perennials for the modern garden than anyone else in Britain. Through his commercial and practical experience he introduced newer, dwarfer species and showed how they could be adapted to smaller borders or Island Beds in a much less formal manner. His own creation, the Dell Garden at Bressingham, has become a mecca for Perennial plant lovers from all over the world. It is of course where I had my early training, both in the garden and nursery. The 5,000 or so species and varieties of Perennials in the Dell Garden is a living museum of plants, continually being enhanced by worthwhile additions from all parts of the world.

Perennial Island Beds in summer at Bressingham

The question of whether a certain plant, be it Perennial, shrub or tree, will be winter hardy in your area or individual garden is of course entirely relative to the geographical area in which you live. In the United States, hardiness zones are available as a guide and plants are categorised according to the minimum temperature which they will tolerate. In Europe and especially in Britain, no such zoning according to hardiness is available, but generally, the cultural information given in this book indicates a plant's suitability for particular situations. It must be noted however, that microclimates can and do exist in certain areas and gardens. For instance, a southern or western facing aspect protected by a garden or house wall will often enable you to grow plants which would be killed in more open, unprotected aspects. Protecting such dormant Perennials with bracken, leaves, straw or hay will also assist.

In the end, though you can seek advice and read books, it is not until you start to experiment yourself that you will discover the pleasures of growing Perennials. Take the recommendations of experts by all means, but the joy and fulfilment from your garden comes from what you put into it. The pleasure of creating a garden, a scene, a bed, a border, or just to see plants thrive and flower, can be yours at very little cost. Why not start now?

Adrian Bloom

What are Perennials?

This term literally means 'perpetual' or 'long lasting' and botanically is a very loose description for what are often referred to as 'Herbaceous' or 'Border Plants'. In this book I am referring to Herbaceous Perennials which are generally accepted as being hardy throughout most of the British Isles (see notes in Preface). Perennials, therefore, are mostly plants which have a longer life than either an Annual which survives just one flowering season or a Biennial which flowers for two seasons. The plants pictured and described in these books on Perennials are neither trees nor shrubs but mostly plants which die right back to the ground in winter to reappear the following spring, and those which will continue to flower year after year.

Why are they good garden plants?

The variety of plants among the range of Hardy Perennials is quite staggering and offers a wide choice to the gardener. There are plants available for almost every situation – for dry shade, for moisture or waterside, for hot sunny banks – you name the area and a plant could be found to fit! Flowers vary tremendously in shape and colour – plants which one might describe as both brash and exquisitely delicate can be found. Foliage should also not be forgotten, as many provide interest long after the flowers are gone. While this book can only be a brief guide to Perennials I hope it will show the variety and versatility among this fascinating group of plants. Lists of plants for Special Purposes (to be found on pages 62–63) will I hope be of help when trying to make a selection for any particular situation in your garden.

How can Perennials best be used in the garden?

Firstly I would suggest one should determine what one wants Perennials for in the garden and then decide where they should be planted. Are plants required to associate with shrubs; for ground-cover purposes or for a splash of colour for as long a period in the year as possible? The list of plants for special purposes will help in the first two instances – but if Perennials are required for a border or bed on their own please first take note of the following paragraphs.

What is a Herbaceous Border?

This is the term referred to a border planted only with Perennials, most often backed by a wall, fence or hedge and which can be viewed only from one side. This one-sided border is still considered the 'conventional' or 'traditional' way of growing Perennials but is to my mind in no way suited to the modern garden and though spectacular on a large scale has considerable disadvantages.

The backing to the border tends to elongate and weaken plants struggling to reach the light and air, leading to the necessity for staking, which is troublesome to say the least. Light and air to produce natural growth are essential to make the most of Perennials. However, it must be agreed that a great many gardens do not allow for anything but a rectangular-shaped border but there are simple rules which if followed will produce much more satisfactory results. The other and, space permitting, more attractive way to plant Perennials for colour is to follow the Island Bed method.

What is an Island Bed?

This method of growing Perennials was first pioneered by my father Alan Bloom some thirty years ago and is now generally accepted as showing Perennials to their best advantage. A round or, better still, irregularly shaped bed is created in a lawn and planted with groups of Perennials in quantities not less than three of a kind. The lowest growing types arranged to suit colour and flowering seasons are towards the front, building up to the taller types in the centre. Careful selection of varieties should mean no staking is required since the groups support each other as they grow and have enough light and air to provide sturdy growth.

Suggested Plans for planting Hardy Perennials

For both Island Beds and conventional rectangular Borders, the main thing to try and achieve is a balance of form and colour for as long a period as possible. The plants in the two plans are my suggestions but, of course, any number of personal selections can be made.

A few notes for guidance: no size is given for bed area since it may vary according to space available. It is suggested no less than three of a variety is used and, where space is available, five or seven will be preferable. Space between different groups should be more than between plants in the same group. Density figures will act as a guide, i.e. *Hosta* 'Royal Standard' D 3–4 will require nearly twice as much space as *Armeria* 'Dusseldorf Pride' D 6. Frontal groups, therefore, will often require less space than the larger plants behind.

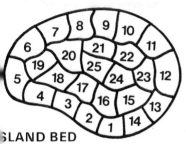

Back

Front

ISLAND BED
Something in flower
from March until October

1. *Hosta fortunei* 'Aureomarginata' D 4
2. *Heuchera* 'Red Spangles' D 5
3. *Aster n-b dwarf* 'Little Pink Beauty' D 5
4. *Anaphalis triplinervis* D 4–5
5. *Sedum* 'Autumn Joy' D 4
6. *Veronica* 'Blue Fountain' D 5
7. *Euphorbia polychroma* D 4–5
8. *Dicentra* 'Adrian Bloom' D 4–5
9. *Coreopsis verticillata* 'Grandiflora' D 5
10. *Tradescantia* 'Purple Dome' D 4–5
11. *Oenothera missouriensis* D 5
12. *Geranium* 'Johnson's Blue' D 5
13. *Doronicum* 'Spring Beauty' D 5
14. *Bergenia cordifolia* 'Purpurea' D 3–4
15. *Lythrum* 'Firecandle' D 4–5
16. *Aconitum Arendsii* D 5–7
17. *Helenium* 'Coppelia' D 5
18. *Scabiosa* 'Clive Greaves' D 5
19. *Solidago* 'Goldenmosa' D 5
20. *Sidalcea* 'Croftway Red' D 5
21. *Eryngium planum* D 5
22. *Hemerocallis* 'Pink Damask' D 4
23. *Hosta* 'Royal Standard' D 3–4
24. *Heliopsis* 'Golden Plume' D 4–5
25. *Miscanthus sinensis* 'Variegatus' D 4

RECTANGULAR
ONE-SIDED BORDER

1. *Phlox paniculata* 'Starfire' D 4–5
2. *Aster × frikartii* D 5
3. *Chrysanthemum maximum* 'Wirral Supreme' D 5
4. *Dictamnus fraxinella* D 5
5. *Hemerocallis* 'Burning Daylight' D 4
6. *Polygonum bistorta* 'Superbum' D 3–4
7. *Campanula lactiflora* 'Prichard's Variety' D 4–5
8. *Monarda* 'Cambridge Scarlet' D 4
9. *Kniphofia* 'Little Maid' D 4
10. *Euphorbia polychroma* D 4–5
11. *Rudbeckia* 'Goldsturm' D 5
12. *Erigeron* 'Adria' D 5
13. *Aster n-b* 'Jenny' D 5
14. *Agapanthus patens* D 4
15. *Crocosmia* 'Spitfire' D 6–7
16. *Achillea* 'Moonshine' D 4–5
17. *Armeria* 'Düsseldorf Pride' D 6
18. *Veronica teucrium* 'Crater Lake Blue' D 5
19. *Potentilla* 'Wm. Rollison' D 5
20. *Pulmonaria* 'Pink Dawn' D 4–5
21. *Geranium* 'Russell Prichard' D 4
22. *Oenothera* 'Fireworks' D 5
23. *Gypsophila* 'Rosy Veil' D 4
24. *Salvia* 'May Night' D 5

A moisture bed in the Dell Gardens at Bressingham. (Left foreground) Astilbe 'Red Sentinel', and (centre) Hosta fortunei 'Aureomarginata'.

What are their likes and dislikes?

There are, as already stated, Perennials to suit every situation. Conversely it can be said that some Perennials do not like certain conditions for which they are not suited! This information is given where applicable within the text describing individual plants and there is also a detailed list of plants for special purposes. However, the majority of Perennials are easily grown in any reasonably friable garden soil – the main requisites being light, air and good drainage, and in some cases, irrigation during summer.

How can one be sure of selecting the best Perennials for the garden?

It should be made clear that some Perennials are grown from seed, others have to be vegetatively propagated, i.e. by splitting, division or by cuttings. Seed-raised plants are not necessarily inferior, very often being young, healthy and vigorous.

However, many of the best and most reliable varieties do not come from seed and in recent years some extremely good dwarfer Perennials have been raised which are particularly suited to the modern garden. Selections have been made to provide plants with a long flowering period, healthy growth and freedom from disease, longevity and ease of maintenance.

My selection of Perennials in this series is made by keeping these factors in mind. The list includes some lesser known but nonetheless worthy plants as well as some of the old favourites. If you want to make the most of Perennials it will certainly be worthwhile to look for some of the better varieties.

When is the best time to plant Perennials?

Late September or early October until late April is the normal season when plants from the open ground can be safely handled. As a general rule early spring flowering plants are best planted in the autumn, late summer or autumn flowering plants in the spring. Some Perennials such as Erigerons, Scabious and Pyrethrums are best planted in spring as are any of a slightly tender nature. However, if plants are grown or sold in pots or containers they are safe to plant almost any time of the year, except in frosty weather, when soil conditions are obviously unsuitable.

Are there any special rules for planting?

If given a position suited to their needs with adequate moisture on planting, Perennials are usually easy to establish but perhaps a reminder should be given on basic principles. Firstly initial preparation of the area to be planted should be made thoroughly. Removal of any perennial weeds is essential as otherwise results will seldom be satisfactory. Perennial weeds and Perennials do not mix!

The soil should be well prepared; compost, peat or farmyard manure, if you are lucky enough to get it, can be added when digging, and will be beneficial, particularly on soils which are either very heavy clay, light and sandy or chalky. A well balanced organic fertiliser will enhance results if added on poor soils once some humus is incorporated.

Good drainage is also essential for success with the great majority of Perennials – few will tolerate waterlogging through winter months – and this is where the importance of deep digging and using humus to open up the structure of the soil is seen. Take care when planting on heavy soils not to tread over the bed during wet periods – use a plank or a board to plant from and always fork over the bed afterwards. Should drainage continue to be a problem, laying drainpipes may be the only answer. Suggestions for planting distances are given with the border and Island Bed Plans. It is important to give adequate spacing between plants and groups of plants.

Planting

Planting should be made with a trowel or a spade, and certainly the latter would be necessary to plant larger bare root plants such as *Papavers* or *Hemerocallis*. Do not plant too deeply – if dormant Perennials should generally have the top of the plant just beneath the surface of the soil, otherwise where roots and shoot meet is usually a reliable guide. Firm each plant well in after insertion but be careful not to overdo it on heavy clay soils! In dry spring periods water distributed to the roots with a watering can and the top drier soil pulled back should provide adequate moisture until the plant is established.

Maintenance and aftercare

Perennial beds will need to be kept free from weeds, particularly before plants become established. If annual weeds are the only problem an occasional hoeing should keep them in check. Hoeing regularly will also be beneficial in preventing moisture loss from the roots in dry weather – moisture essential to young new growth.

In the late autumn when flowers are finished, flower heads and remaining foliage should be trimmed to within a few inches of the ground, and areas between plants forked over if weeds have appeared or the soil is compacted. Compost can be added if required. Some Perennials such as Michaelmas Daisies may need replanting every three or four years if growth becomes too congested. Always select younger outside growths to replant, and discard old material.

Trouble free plants is a relative term – Perennials are certainly less trouble than many. We do not expect in life to get something for nothing and this rule applies to gardening also. A little effort applied at the correct time should without a doubt give increased pleasure from your Perennials – year after year.

Some of the best Perennials

The list of subjects which follows is by no means exhaustive and from the wide range of varieties to choose from some favourites may be left out. Reliability, adaptability and distinction have been the guidelines I have tried to follow when making a choice.

Some people may find Latin names confusing but there is no easy way round that one; what is recognised in one part of the country under a 'Common Name' may be known under quite a different name in another. Latin names usually describe the plant admirably enough and are internationally recognised, so unavoidably we are stuck with them!

Lastly, please note the use of the letter D and a number after each plant described. This denotes a planting density per square metre. D 3 would mean, for example, 3 plants to the square metre are suggested because the plant is vigorous, and D 6, 6 plants to the square metre should be used where a plant is smaller and perhaps less vigorous.

Heights where given are only approximate as growth may vary according to soils, positioning and climatic conditions.

Acanthus

Deep-rooted plants which associate well with shrubs. They prefer sun and good drainage and will withstand drought extremely well.

Acanthus spinosus. A spectacular plant with dark green deeply cut spiny leaves. Flowers of rose-purple open on stiff 150 cm spikes above a canopy of leaves. The flowers appear in June and remain during August – a most effective architectural and foliage plant. D 3–4.

Achillea

Easy-growing plants ranging from small Alpine types to Perennials of some stature. All prefer sun and good drainage, some of the more silvery, woolly-foliaged types succumbing to winter wet. Most are useful for cutting and drying.

Achillea 'Coronation Gold'. A reliable Perennial with a flowering period from June

Acanthus spinosus.

Achillea *'Moonshine'*.

Aconitum *'Bressingham Spire'*.

Agapanthus patens.

Alchemilla mollis.

until September. Green foliage with erect 90 cm stems bearing yellow flat-headed flowers. Good for cutting and drying. D 4.

***Achillea millefolium* 'Cerise Queen'.** A useful variety with bright cerise flat-headed flowers from June until August. Growth is a bit open but fairly vigorous, reaching 60 cm. D 4.

***Achillea* 'Moonshine'.** Without doubt and deservedly the most popular *Achillea*. Dwarf in habit, reaching about 60 cm, with bright silvery foliage through most of the year followed by light yellow almost glistening flowers from June until August. D 4–5.

Aconitum

Known commonly as 'Monks Hood', Aconitums are poisonous but only in the unlikely event of them being eaten. Though adaptable to sun or semi-shade they will not give of their best where too dry or starved. A mulch of compost or fertilised peat will be beneficial in overcoming any shyness to flower which may occur when plants become too congested. Groups should be thinned out every few years and replanted.

***Aconitum* 'Bressingham Spire'.** This is a first-class plant of sturdy symmetrical habit; its tapering 90 cm spikes carry deep green glossy foliage and deep violet-blue flowers in July and August. D 6–7.

***Aconitum carmichaelii* 'Arendsii'.** An easy and reliable 'Monks Hood' growing strongly to 125 cm, the stiffly held spikes producing hooded flowers of an intense steel-blue during September and October. D 5–7.

***Aconitum septentrionale* 'Ivorine'.** A neat growing plant with attractive white flowers borne on dense 90 cm bushes from May to July. D 4–5.

Agapanthus

The 'African Lily' family includes many species not hardy in all except the mildest districts in the British Isles, but those listed below have proved themselves reliably hardy and indispensable Perennials. Requiring sun and good drainage and perhaps, in very cold districts, a covering in winter with leaves or bracken, Agapanthus *will flower happily for years without disturbance. Useful as tub plants, but used as such they should not be allowed to become too dry in summer – a factor also applying to plants in the open ground. Extremely useful and popular subjects for flower arranging.*

***Agapanthus campanulatus* 'Isis'.** Typical strap-like leaves, clusters of dark blue flowers on narrow rounded 75 cm stems. Flowers appear in July and last into August. A most striking plant. D 5.

A. c. 'Headbourne Hybrids'. A fine strain of hardy *Agapanthus* giving a range of colours from pale china to deep violet-blue. Heights may vary also, since these are

9

Anemone japonica
'September Charm'.

Artemisia 'Silver Queen'.

Aquilegia 'Biedermierer'.

raised from seed, but are likely to be within the 60–120 cm mark. Flowering period is July and August. A group of these will provide an interesting feature as *Agapanthus* associate well with other Perennials, shrubs or on their own in isolation. D 4.
A. c. patens. A plant of real merit with large clustered heads of clear light blue on 90 cm stems. Free flowering, giving colour from July until early September. D 4.

Alchemilla

Alchemilla mollis. A useful and attractive Perennial which is adaptable to both sun and shade. This species has large light green Pelargonium-like leaves and soft yellow-green flowers from June until August. It is by no means a spectacular plant but associates well with shrubs or at the front of a bed or border. Reaching only 45 cm it makes an excellent ground-cover plant where not too dry. D 4–5.

Anaphalis

There are several species and varieties of this easily grown Perennial but many are rather similar. All have silvery-green leaves and white 'Everlasting Flowers' and thrive on almost any soils, preferring sun but putting up with some shade. Good foliage plants and excellent used as contrast against bright colourful subjects.

Anaphalis triplinervis. The most attractive species, forming neat bushes 30 cm high with silvery leaves and white flowers. An improved form recently introduced from Germany is called 'Summer Snow' which is even brighter as a foliage plant. Both D 4–5.

Anemone

Anemone japonica. *'The Japanese Anemones' are first-class late flowering plants for Perennial beds or borders, spreading by underground roots but not invasive. Growing best in sun, they will nonetheless do equally well in some shade. Pot-grown plants establish best but they do not always give their best show until a year after planting. Some of the new varieties are particularly striking. All have saucer-shaped flowers from 6 to 10 cm across, and appear in August and last through until October, depending somewhat on weather and soil conditions.*

Anemone japonica **'September Charm'**. Single flowers of soft pink with golden-yellow centres. Growing to 45 cm, this variety has a most charming and graceful habit and is deservedly popular. D 4.

10

A. j. **'White Queen'** is a recent introduction with larger flowers and more luxuriant growth than the older yet ever popular 'Louise Uhink.' Both make their mark in the autumn with clear snow-white flowers. Taller than the pinks, reaching 90–100 cm. D 5.

Aquilegia

Commonly known as 'Columbine', there are in fact a great many species and varieties of different shapes and sizes in this family. Most come from seed and are relatively short lived but quite showy nonetheless in their flowering period, which is usually during May and June. Not fussy as to soils but preferring sun and good drainage.

Aquilegia **'Biedermeier'.** A seedling strain of German origin with upraised flower heads of varying shades. Heights also vary from 30–45 cm. An unusual and attractive plant for a frontal position in the bed or border. D 5.

Aquilegia **'McKana Hybrids'.** The most popular, colourful and reliable strain of 'Columbine' which provides a wide range of flower colours and combinations. These flowers come in reds, pinks, blues and yellows and attain 5–10 cm in width on stems reaching between 70–90 cm. The flowering period is slightly later than most Aquilegias, from June until August. D 5.

Armeria

Though many of the 'Thrift' family should probably be classed as Alpine plants, the more robust and reliable types have a definite place at the front of the border or in a dwarf Island Bed. Most are easy to grow, preferring sun and good drainage. In wet conditions they are likely to be short lived.

Armeria latifolia **'Bees Ruby'.** An outstanding plant with glistening rosy-pink rounded flowers from June until August above tufts of thin strap-like leaves of bright green. This is the tallest of the Armerias at 40 cm and not always an easy transplanter from the open ground so pot-grown plants are preferable. D 3.

Armeria maritima **'Alba'.** A worthwhile Perennial making hummocks of green leaves from which appear contrasting white flowers 15 cm high during mid to late summer. D 5.

A. m. **'Dusseldorf Pride'** (Düsseldorffer Stolz'). A new but well-proven continental variety of great merit with deep rosy-red flowers on 15 cm stems. Very free flowering from June until August on neat rounded evergreen hummocks. D 6.

Artemisia

While colourful Perennials make the most show, they can often be shown to better advantage when used carefully in association with not only contrasting colours but contrasting foliage. This is where such plants as Artemisias come in since they are

Armeria maritima *'Dusseldorf Pride'.*

Anaphalis triplinervis.

mostly silver and grey leaved. Some are rather shrubby in nature, some somewhat invasive but all have aromatic foliage. As one might imagine with silver-foliaged plants they dislike wet, badly drained situations and although fairly tolerant of shade prefer sun and good drainage.

Artemisia absinthium. A useful clump-forming plant with silver leaves, particularly attractive in early spring, followed by whitish flowers on 90 cm bushes. D 4.

    A. a. 'Lambrook Silver'. A reliable semi-shrubby type which produces abundant silvery-grey foliage on 90 cm bushes, and sprays of greyish flowers in summer. D 4.

Artemisia 'Silver Queen'. Although inclined to be slightly invasive this is the most silvery and most reliable of the grey-leaved herbaceous types. The foliage reaches 75 cm with thin silver-grey leaves and whitish-grey flowers of little distinction. D 5.

Aruncus

Aruncus sylvester. Perhaps not a plant for every garden but it is a most distinctive perennial for soils not lacking in moisture. The attractive abundant foliage in spring produces by June luxuriant creamy-white plumes reaching an imposing 150 cm. Ideal for moisture or waterside where conditions will extend the rather brief flowering period, this plant will need some space for development. D 3.

Aster

This is a large family of popular garden plants which includes the well-known 'Michaelmas Daisies'. There are, of course, many lesser known but equally garden-worthy species, some of which can be briefly mentioned. Most are reliable and long lived if given sun and good drainage but special requirements are given where relevant.

Aster amellus. First-class plants requiring good drainage and reasonable soil conditions for best results. Open-ground plants should be planted in spring but pot grown are safe in autumn. All have single-rayed daisy-like flowers with yellow centres and, with the exception of *A. × frikartii* which is a hybrid, all flower from August until October. Some of the best varieties are:

    A. a. 'Brilliant'. Bright pink flowers on 75 cm stems. A good reliable grower. D 5.

    A. a. 'King George'. One of the oldest and most popular varieties with violet-blue flowers. A little dwarfer at 60 cm. D 5.

    A. a. 'Violet Queen'. ('Veilchen Königin'). An outstanding introduction from Germany. Very free flowering violet, dwarf and compact habit to only 45 cm. D 5.

    A. × frikartii has *A. amellus* as one parent and *A. thomsonii* as another. The resulting seedling which arose in Switzerland many years ago is one of the finest

Aster novi-belgii *'Patricia Ballard'*.

Aster novi-belgii *'Jenny'*.

A field of 'Michaelmas Daisies' in full flower during October.

Aster×frikartii.

Perennials of all time. Large light lavender-blue flowers top 90 cm bushes from July to October. Once established it will give pleasure for years with little attention. D 5.

Aster novi-belgii. The 'Michaelmas Daisies' are still favourites as garden Perennials despite some drawbacks. Many of the larger-flowered and taller varieties have been superseded by dwarfer, bushier ones which are less prone to flop untidily. Some of the newer varieties are also less susceptible to wilt and mildew. Even so most will be better for dividing and replanting every three or four years to maintain vigour and flower size. Nevertheless, there are few plants which can offer such a wide colour range late in the year, and I believe some of the following varieties should deserve a place in the garden. All flower during September and October.

A. n-b. **'Blandie'.** Pure white semi-double. Rather tall, 120 cm. D 4.

A. n-b. **'Carnival'.** Erect habit, semi-double cherry-red flowers. 60 cm. D 5.

A. n-b. **'Marie Ballard'.** A reliable first-class variety with fine double light blue flowers. 90 cm. D 5.

A. n-b. **'Patricia Ballard'.** Semi-double rich pink flowers. 90 cm. D 5.

A. n-b. **'Percy Thrower'.** Double deep blue. 90 cm. D 5.

A. n-b. **'Raspberry Ripple'.** A descriptive name for a recent introduction. Double carmine-red. 75 cm. D 5.

A. n-b. **'Winston S. Churchill'.** Perhaps the most popular variety of all time. Large semi-double flowers of rich purple-red on erect stems. 75 cm. D 5.

Aster novi-belgii – Dwarf Varieties. Excellent for front of the border positions, making mounded compact bushes and more suited to the modern smaller garden. Otherwise similar cultural conditions are required.

A. n-b. **'Audrey'.** Single mauve-blue flowers on 40 cm stems. A good reliable free-flowering variety. D 5–6.

A. n-b. **'Jenny'.** An excellent introduction with double violet-purple flowers. 30 cm. D 5.

A. n-b. **'Little Pink Beauty'.** Without doubt one of the best of all 'Michaelmas Daisies'. Semi-double clear pink. 40 cm. D 5.

A. n-b. **'Snowsprite'.** Mounded bushes produce masses of pure white semi-double flowers. 30 cm. D 5.

Aster thomsonii 'Nana'. An attractive dwarf and neat growing *Aster* which produces delicate lavender-blue flowers from July until October. Grows to about 45 cm and requires good drainage for longevity. D 5–6.

13

Astilbe

Though often wrongly referred to as Spirea, *now a separate genus, the* Astilbe *must be classed as a classic Hardy Perennial. Astilbes usually prefer conditions where moisture exists and perhaps slight shade but they will also grow quite successfully in normal garden soil which is not impoverished or subject to drying out. Long lived and trouble free they will certainly flower for a longer period where ample moisture and some shade exists. With their graceful cut and arching foliage and plumes of white, pinks and reds, the Astilbes somehow offer a touch of class to the garden despite their lack of adaptability. A selection of some of the best varieties follows. Most flower from late June until August.*

Astilbe × arendsii 'Bressingham Beauty'. A popular variety with well-formed spikes of rich pink on 75 to 90 cm stems. D 4.

A. × a. 'Federsee'. Perhaps the most adaptable to less moist conditions. Bright rosy-red plumes to 60 cm. D 4.

A. × a. 'Fanal'. A reliable form with striking deep red plumes 60 cm in height. D 5.

A. × a. 'Irrlicht'. Like the preceding two varieties an introduction from Germany. This is the best white-flowered variety, with contrasting dark green foliage. 60 cm. D 5.

A. × a. 'Montgomery'. Perhaps the deepest red. 60 cm. D 5.

Astilbe simplicifolia 'Atrorosea'. A popular dwarf variety which produces striking plumes of deep glowing pink. 45–60 cm. D 5.

A. s. 'Sprite'. A Bressingham introduction of greatest merit. It has deeply cut dark green foliage from which emerge plumes of bright shell-pink flowers to about 25 cm. D 5.

Astilbe sinensis 'Pumila'. A strong-growing dwarf form of great merit with short compact 30 cm spikes of lilac-rose from July until September. D 5.

Astilbe taquetii 'Superba'. A majestic plant with large spikes of bright rose-lilac flowers from July until September. 120 cm. D 4.

Astrantia

Unusual plants which have become more valued in recent years because of their popularity for flower arranging. Adaptable to most soils they prefer some moisture and light shade. In such conditions they produce abundant foliage and flowers which are distinctive for their effect and appearance rather than for their colour.

Astilbe × arendsii *'Federsee'.* Astilbe simplicifolia *'Sprite'.*

Astrantia 'Rubra'.

Bergenia cordifolia 'Purpurea'.

Bergenia 'Ballawley'.

***Astrantia carniolica* 'Major'.** The strongest-growing form, with attractively cut leaves and large pinkish-green flower bracts on 90 cm stems. These last from June until August and are invaluable for flower arrangers. D 4.

   ***A. c.* 'Rubra'.** A compact variety with deep crimson-green flowers and bracts from June until September. 45 cm. D 5.

Astrantia involucrata. A beautiful free-flowering plant with heads of green and white. Flowers start in June and last until October. Perhaps the best for flower arranging. 75 cm. D 4.

Bergenia

An 'Old Fashioned' Perennial which has come back to popularity in recent years due to improved colours of new varieties and because of their adaptability and use as ground-cover plants. All have typical large, rounded leathery leaves and flower spikes, seldom exceeding 60 cm, which appear during the March to May period.

***Bergenia* 'Ballawley'.** One of the new hybrids with large glossy green leaves and 30 cm spikes of bright rose-red flowers which can unfortunately be susceptible to spring frosts. D 3.

***Bergenia cordifolia* 'Purpurea'.** The best for ground cover with broad heart-shaped leaves which remain close to the ground, and drooping sprays of pink flowers on 25 cm spikes. D 3–4.

***Bergenia* 'Evening Glow'.** ('Abendglut'). A choice variety with dark rosy-red flowers to 30 cm. D 5.

***Bergenia* 'Bressingham White'.** This is an improvement on B. 'Silberlicht' (Silver Light), being freer flowering, more robust and a purer white. 30–40 cm. Both are worth having. D 4.

Caltha palustris *'Plena'*.   Campanula lactiflora *'Prichard's Variety'*.

Caltha

Although these 'Marsh Marigolds' are usually classed as waterside plants they are nonetheless indispensable for those gardens with moist conditions.

Caltha palustris 'Plena'. This is a true harbinger of spring with its bright double flowers of pure golden yellow from March until May. 30 cm. D 5.

Campanula

The 'Bell Flower' family, includes some of the smallest of Alpine species to robust Perennials of two metres in height. Those useful for Island Beds or borders only are described here. Some of the less well-known species and varieties are certainly worthy of wider recognition. Most prefer sun and well-drained soil but some also grow very well in light shade.

Campanula alliarifolia 'Ivory Bells'. Is one of those which tolerates shade and is a reliable and attractive Perennial. It has hairy leaves and arching 50 cm stems carrying dangling ivory-white flowers from June until August. D 5.

Campanula carpatica. This and its varieties are some of the most useful front of the border subjects and provide a carpeting effect even when not in flower. All grow 20–30 cm and flower in the June–August period, and give a better account of themselves in lighter loamy soils. A few of the best varieties are listed below.

  C. c. **'Blue Moonlight'.** Has large cups of light blue. D 5–6.

  C. c. **'Bressingham White'.** Large clear white flowers make a pleasant contrast to the green foliage. D 5–6.

  C. c. **'Chewton Joy'.** An outstanding variety with saucer-like china-blue flowers flowering somewhat later than other varieties. D 6–7.

Campanula poscharskyana 'Stella'. A first-rate Perennial for a frontal position although it, like the carpaticas, is usually classed as an Alpine or Rock Plant. Quite vigorous and spreading though not invasive, with small star-like blue flowers on dark green bushes through June until August. It reaches 15–20 cm. D 5–6.

Campanula glomerata 'Superba'. A strong growing and reliable 'Bellflower' which makes quite a show in the garden during June and July with bright violet-blue flowers on 75 cm stems. Tends to need restraining on rich soils. D 4–5.

Campanula lactiflora. Is very variable when grown from seed but some excellent named selections have been introduced which I would recommend as the best buy. All are easy and reliably perennial, adapting well to shade as well as sun, moist soils as well as dry.

C. I. **'Alba'**. Although spectacular in a position where space can be found this attractive form at 120–150 cm is likely to be rather tall for most modern gardens. Masses of bell-shaped flowers appear up the stems from June until August. D 4.

C. I. **'Loddon Anna'**. A variety with pinkish flowers and a similar height and habit to 'Alba'. D 4.

C. I. **'Pouffe'**. One of the first new introductions to be raised by my father this is a distinctive miniature form with a rounded mound-like habit only 25 cm high which is covered in masses of lavender-blue flowers from June until September. D 4–5.

C. I. **'Prichard's Variety'**. The best selected deep blue with a sturdy bushy habit reaching 90 cm, a much better height for the present-day garden. Flowers appear in June lasting until August. D 4–5.

Campanula persicifolia. This species is one of the most common 'Bell Flowers' used for herbaceous borders but also is one of the most variable and short lived. Some of the selected forms also have these characteristics but 'Telham Beauty' is a reliable and distinctive exception. It has large rich blue cup-shaped flowers produced in profusion on 130–140 cm stems from June to August. D 5.

Catananche

Catananche coerulea. An easy-growing plant raised mostly from seed but a useful Perennial, particularly on warm dry soils. In fact sun and good drainage are essential to this sometimes short-lived plant. Greyish-green leaves and 60 cm narrow stems are tipped by bright blue 'Cornflowers' from June to late summer. The flowers respond well to drying and are indispensable for flower arrangers. D 5.

Centaurea

Some of this family of Perennials are really unsuitable for all but the larger garden but some of the most useful and reliable plants for general use are mentioned below. Most prefer sun but generally are adaptable to soils.

Centaurea dealbata **'John Coutts'**. A beautiful free-flowering Perennial with grey-green leaves and large bright pink cornflower heads. Growing 60 cm high the flowers are carried from May until August with the peak in June. Both this and the next

A colourful conventional border in midsummer. Centaurea *'John Coutts'.*

variety can be invasive on rich moist soils where abundant growth may be made at the expense of flower. D 4.

C. d. 'Steenbergii'. Similar in form and habit to 'John Coutts' this variety has silver-grey foliage, but its rosy-red flowers, which appear in June and last until August, are carried on 75 cm stems. D 4.

Chrysanthemum

This genus covers a very wide range of plants of which only a few are reliably perennial. The most useful and popular Perennial in this family is Chrysanthemum maximum *and even some varieties of this species are unsatisfactory, often being unreliable and short lived. Some dwarfer varieties show promise.*

Chrysanthemum maximum 'Wirral Supreme'. Without a doubt the most reliable, and luckily one of the most attractive varieties! Robust in habit with dark green leaves and large semi-double white flowers, it makes an impressive display. The flowers are borne on 90 cm stems from July until September and are excellent for cutting, while the pure white make an effective contrast to more colourful Perennials. D 5.

Cimicifuga

Graceful in habit and stately when in flower these are plants which prefer good soils and some shade but not too dry.

Cimicifuga cordifolia. Dark, deeply cut foliage provides a pleasant impression long before the slender branching spikes of creamy white appear in August. These, reaching 120 cm, last for several weeks. There are some other somewhat similar and equally useful species and varieties in cultivation. D 4.

Coreopsis

Some species of this family are unreliably perennial. However, Coreopsis verticillata *'Grandiflora' mentioned below is both hardy and long lived and certainly in my list of top ten Perennials.*

Coreopsis verticillata 'Grandiflora'. One of the most rewarding of Perennials, forming neat bushes of green which open in July to masses of golden-yellow star-like flowers and last until September. With a maximum height of 60 cm this is an ideal plant for the smaller garden, its only preference being for sun and its only dislike poor barren soils. D 5.

Left: Cimicifuga cordifolia.
Below: Coreopsis verticillata *'Grandiflora'*.

Crocosmia masonorum.

Crocosmia 'Ember Glow'.

Crocosmia

Closely related to Montbretia *and* Antholyza. *The species* masonorum, *which is a South African plant, has, since its introduction to this country, added colour to many gardens. More recently at Bressingham* Crocosmia masonorum *has been successfully crossed with both* Montbretia *and* Antholyza *to produce some startling new hybrids. All the types listed below have corm-like roots which after some time form matted clusters and may need thinning and replanting every few years. All prefer warm, well-drained soils and are trouble free. In cold districts a covering of leaves, straw or bracken will ensure plants coming through the winter unscathed but most British winters do not provide a threat to their hardiness.*

Crocosmia **'Ember Glow'.** This cross between *C. masonorum* and *Antholyza paniculata* has glowing dusky-orange red flowers on sprays 75 cm in height. These appear in July lasting for several weeks, and like other Crocosmias this is a most useful subject for flower arranging. D 6–7.

Crocosmia **'Spitfire'.** This cross between *C. masonorum* and *Montbretia* is a brilliant new introduction with fiery orange flowers on wiry stems – height 75 cm. Like 'Ember Glow' it is vigorous in growth, flowering in July and August. D 6–7.

Crocosmia masonorum. Perhaps, being a parent of both the above, this should have come first! To my mind it is still not used enough in gardens, being a showy and easy plant requiring little maintenance, beyond thinning out the corms every few years. Hardy, its bright green foliage erupts into flower in July with bright orange sprays on graceful arching 60 cm stems. Since this plant can be seed raised both superior and inferior strains are in circulation. D 7–9.

Delphinium

Long known as the 'Queen of the Border' Delphiniums have suffered a decline in popularity in recent years since most are not trouble free, and though spectacular some of the tall large-flowered hybrids are unsuitable for the smaller garden. Where one is prepared to take the trouble of preparing and manuring the soil, protecting from slugs in winter and staking in summer they can be a very rewarding sight. However, to my mind a less expensive method for those who like Delphiniums is to grow the varieties which come from seed or to go for the dwarfer more perennial but less stately Belladonna Hybrid varieties.

Delphinium **Belladonna Hybrids. 'Blue Bees'.** Light glacier-blue flowers from June until August on branching 120 cm spikes. D 4.

   D. Belladonna Hybrids. 'Peace'. Intense deep blue, a reliable grower with similar height and habit to 'Blue Bees'. D 4.

   D. Belladonna Hybrid. 'Pink Sensation'. Not robust but most effective when grown well with rose-pink flowers to 90 cm from June to August. D 4–5.

Large-flowered Hybrids. Although many strains can be bought and raised from seed or the seedling plants themselves purchased, without doubt the best strain is Blackmore and Langdons. This produces strong healthy plants in a wide range of colours. Variation in height is likely also, between 120 and 200 cm but all are likely to flower during June and July with sometimes a later crop on young plants. D 5.

Dianthus

The 'Hardy Border Pinks' are always worth growing for both flower and foliage. Requiring well-drained soil and sun, they may need rejuvenating every few years since there is a tendency to become old and leggy in time. Most have scented flowers, a distinct attraction.

Dianthus 'Emperor'. Double crimson flowers to 30 cm from May until July. D 4–5.

Dianthus 'Excelsior'. Also known as 'Pink Mrs Sinkins', like that old and well-known variety it is a beautifully scented double-flowered type with narrow silver-grey leaves. The rose-pink flowers are borne on 15–25 cm stems in June and July. D 4–5.

Dianthus 'Mrs Sinkins'. The ever-popular 'Cottage Garden' variety with double white scented flowers. Similar in habit to 'Excelsior' flowering in June and July. D 4–5.

Dicentra

Attractive perennials with fleshy roots and deeply cut delicate foliage. Most types like reasonably moist but well-drained soils and succeed in sun and some shade.

Dicentra eximia 'Adrian Bloom'. I would have some hesitation in describing a plant which bears my name were it not such a good Perennial! Raised and named by

Delphinium *Mixed Hybrids.*   Dicentra spectabilis.

Dicentra *'Adrian Bloom'*. Doronicum *'Spring Beauty'*. Dictamnus fraxinella.

my father Alan Bloom (for whom I am still looking for a plant to give his name) this has proved itself over several years. Crimson pendulous flowers on 30 cm stems are produced in abundance during April and May over rich green finely cut foliage. Equal in merit is the U.S.A. introduction 'Luxuriant'. D 4–5.

Dicentra spectabilis. A popular garden Perennial known under descriptive common names such as 'Bleeding Heart' and 'Dutchman's Breeches'. Requiring good soil which is moist yet well drained, this can be a most rewarding plant. Heart-shaped pink and white lockets hang prettily from arching stems during April and May. Flowers are at their peak before the luxuriant light green foliage takes over. High winds and spring frosts can be a trial to early growth. D 4.

Dictamnus

'The Burning Bush' is a choice and trouble-free Perennial which is reliable and long lived though sometimes slow to establish. They require good drainage and a sunny position, associating well with both Perennials and Shrubs.

Dictamnus fraxinella. Erect bushes produce spikes of lilac flowers 75 cm high from June until August. D 5.

   D. f. **'Alba'**. Almost more spectacular than the more common *D. fraxinella* this is a little-known plant with bright pure white flowers contrasting strongly against dark green foliage. The same height, habit and flowering period as the species. D 5.

Doronicum

An easy-growing genus of spring-flowering plants which add a fresh brightness to the garden when most required. Put in full sun for best effect, but partial shade and almost any soil will also give good results. As with most spring-flowering Perennials which need rejuvenating, division should be made in early autumn.

Doronicum caucasicum **'Spring Beauty'** ('Frühlingspracht'). One of my favourite harbingers of spring with its bright double yellow flowers contrasting beautifully with the fresh green foliage. Flowers are borne during April and May on 30 cm stems – an ideal height for the smaller garden, bed or border. A must for the top ten of Hardy Perennials, though often difficult to find. D 5.

Doronicum **'Miss Mason'**. Probably the best single dwarf variety with bright yellow rayed flowers on 45 cm stems from April until June. D 5.

Echinacea *'B. Hybrids'*.   Eryngium bourgatii.   Erigeron *'Foerster's Liebling'*.

Echinacea

Formerly classed under the Rudbeckia genus these are known as the 'Purple Cone Flowers', though there is now a white form – which could perhaps invalidate that name! All like well-drained soils but at the same time dislike extremely dry conditions. They are mostly long lived and reliable.

Echinacea purpurea 'Bressingham Hybrids'. This strain of seedlings are much improved over the ordinary *E. Purpurea*, having a sturdy upright habit with large glowing purple-red flowers on 90 cm stems from July until early September. D 5.

   E. p. 'The King'. An old favourite and still a reliable Perennial with large purple-crimson flowers as much as 10 cm across and drooping petals. The flowering period is from July until September on 110 cm stems – perhaps height is its only drawback. D 5.

   E. p. 'White Lustre'. An attractive though not spectacular white version of the 'Cone Flower'. Also reaching 90 cm and flowering from mid to late summer. D 5.

Epimedium

These early spring-flowering plants bear delicate flowers of different colours, while most are also useful in providing ground cover with their attractive leaves. All are mat forming, preferring light shade for best effect but growing well in most soils, heavy or light, moist or comparatively dry.

Epimedium macranthum 'Rose Queen'. A beautiful form with light green foliage and deep pink flowers which continue from April until early June on 15 cm stems. D 5.

Epimedium perralderianum. More evergreen than some – the serrated light green leaves make a pretty contrast to the bright yellow flowers during April and May. The height is 25 cm. D 5.

Epimedium rubrum. This is one of the most attractive and reliable species, making a carpet of fresh green and bronzed leaves following a show of flowers during April and May on 25 cm stems. Delicate crimson flowers, like the carpet of leaves, reach 25–30 cm. D 5.

Erigeron

A genus whose flowers closely resemble the Asters of 'Michaelmas Daisies' although both the flowering period and habits are quite different. Recently introduced plants from Bressingham and Germany have vastly improved flower colour, size and plant vigour over earlier raised varieties. Many still have a lax habit in flower, though it is true that the season of flowering is a long one. Erigerons are usually long lived and adaptable to soils, preferring sun and reasonable drainage. Spring division is recommended. Some, though certainly not all, of the best varieties are described.

Erigeron **'Adria'**. Is a recent introduction from Germany with rich lavender-blue flowers held on erect 75 cm stems and flowering from June until August. D 5.

Erigeron **'Charity'**. A clear light pink, one of the Bressingham-raised 'ity' range. Flowers are borne at 60 cm from June until August. D 5.

Erigeron **'Foerster's Liebling'**. Perhaps the best and certainly the most popular *Erigeron*. Large semi-double deep pink flowers on compact 50 cm bushes provide a beautiful show through June, July and into August. D 5.

Erigeron **'Prosperity'**. A reliable light blue semi-double variety. Height and flowering period similar to 'Foerster's Liebling'. D 5.

Eryngium

Distinctive and unusual plants popular with flower arrangers for their often metallic-blue flowers heads and spiny stems and leaves. All like well-drained soils and prefer sunny positions.

Eryngium bourgatii. This dwarf species originating from the Pyrenees has deeply cut silvery-blue leaves with whitish markings. Light blue flower heads from above bract-like 45 cm stems lasting from June until August. D 6.

Eryngium oliverianum. An intricate branching system produces attractive spiny blue flowers reaching 90 cm, in contrast to deep green deeply cut leaves. A reliable variety giving a good show from June through to August. D 5.

Eryngium planum. A strong growing and reliable form with bright blue flowers on 90 cm stems. Flowering from June until August, it is excellent for cutting. D 5.

Euphorbia

In recent years the 'Spurge' family have enjoyed increasing popularity and with good reason. Most are of easy cultivation, long lived and reliable, offering both attractive flowers or bracts and foliage over a long period. Nonetheless, some provide more for the average gardener than others and it is those which are described below.

Euphorbia griffithii **'Fireglow'**. A startling sight in early summer when its bract-like flowers show fiery orange-red on 60 cm stems. This early flush of colour gradually loses intensity, and is overtaken by a further 15 cm of lush green bushy growth. Spreading underground stems do not usually become invasive. D 4–5.

Euphorbia myrsinites. A most striking plant for a frontal position. Trailing stems carry leaves of blue-grey terminating in large yellow flower heads during May and June. Like most Euphorbias it will tolerate sun or part shade. D 4–5.

Euphorbia polychroma. Also still known as *E. epithymoides*, this plant is another one could include in the top ten Perennials. Sulphur-yellow bracts develop slowly in spring from clumps of purple-green shoots. Neat rounded bushes grow in stature, displaying flowers from early April until late May when the foliage will reach its full height at 45 cm. A Perennial with all the virtues! D 4–5.

Euphorbia epithymoides.   Euphorbia griffithii *'Fireglow'*.

Gaillardia

Though well known and popular Perennials, Gaillardias are not without faults. Rich bright flowers last for long periods but plants can be short lived, disliking poor drainage and heavy soils. Full sun and good drainage is essential for full rewards. Seed-raised collections usually contain variations of colour and I would recommend the two distinct named varieties below, both of which are excellent for cutting.

Gaillardia **'Croftway Yellow'**. A well-proven variety with large clear bright yellow flowers on 75 cm stems from June until September. D 5.
Gaillardia **'Mandarin'**. Flowers of orange flame make a striking display from June until August on 90 cm stems. D 5.

Geranium

The true Geraniums include some of the most versatile and hardy of Perennials. Most grow happily on a wide range of soils and are adaptable to shady situations. Unfortunately, only a few of the wide range of species and varieties can be mentioned here. Most are clump forming and drought resistant.

Geranium armenum. Large cut leaves, bushy growth to 90 cm produces large vivid magenta flowers during June and July. D 4.
Geranium endressii **'Wargrave Pink'**. This and the very similar 'Arthur Johnson' are first-class plants for ground cover, growing vigorously in sun or part shade with an abundance of bright green foliage to 40 cm. This is spotted with clear pink flowers from June through until September. D 4.
Geranium **'Johnson's Blue'**. A popular hybrid with bright lavender blue cup shaped flowers on 45 cm bushes from May until August. D 5.
Geranium **'Russell Prichard'**. This, like so many other good Perennials, has stood the test of time and remains one of the best. Low growing in habit to 25 cm the grey-green lobed leaves set off intense carmine-red flowers from June until early September. D 4.
Geranium sanguineum. Another low-growing species with small leaves and magenta-purple flowers during mid to late summer. D 4.
G. s. lancastrense **'Splendens'**. This long and tiresome name hides a very good garden plant. Creeping habit to 25 cm similar to *sanguineum*, gives a continuous show of light rose-pink flowers from June until September. D 4.

Geranium *'Russell Prichard'*. Geranium armenum.

A good example of an Island Bed with plants being self-supporting. (Foreground) Gypsophila paniculata 'Compacta Plena'.

Geum borisii.

Geum

This small group of species and varieties include some of the brightest flowered of Perennials, though some are short lived. All prefer sun and good drainage and may require dividing every few years to maintain vigour and longevity.

Geum borisii. A reliable hybrid with neat tufted bright green foliage, producing intense orange flowers on slender 30 cm stems from May and often lasting through until early September. D 5.

Geum 'Georgenberg'. Has single deep yellow flowers only 30 cm high over compact leafy clumps. A first-class front of the border plant, flowering from April until June. D 6.

Geum 'Lady Stratheden'. This, with bright double yellow flowers, and 'Mrs Bradshaw', its semi-double red counterpart, are the best known and possibly most colourful varieties. Both, however, are seed raised and fairly short lived if a true Perennial is required. Both reach 60 cm and flower during mid to late summer. D 5.

Gypsophila

'Baby's Breath'. Gypsophila paniculata and its varieties make a wonderful show with their myriads of tiny flowers in well-drained conditions. The larger varieties also tend to take up rather a lot of space and to my mind are not really suitable subjects for most gardens.

Gypsophila paniculata 'Compacta Plena'. Makes a marvellous show of small white flowers on 45 cm bushes from June until August. A good foil for brighter colours and useful for cutting. D 4.

G. p. 'Rosy Veil'. Much dwarfer at about 25 cm and with its mound-like habit and masses of double pink button flowers from June until September rates as a first-class Perennial. Good drainage is essential for longevity. D 4.

25

Helenium 'Coppelia'.   Helenium 'Golden Youth'.

Helenium

These Perennials are among the most showy and rewarding, particularly in some of the newer more compact varieties. All are clump forming and may need thinning every few years to retain vigour and flower size. They prefer good drainage and an open sunny position. Only a few varieties can be mentioned here.

Helenium 'Bressingham Gold'. A striking variety of recent introduction. Growing to 90 cm, with a sturdy branching system, it has flowers of deep gold suffused crimson during July and August. D 4–5.

Helenium 'Coppelia'. Without a doubt one of the best. Raised at Bressingham it has quickly become popular. Flowers of a glowing coppery orange on 90 cm stems during July and August make a marvellous show. D 5.

Helenium 'Golden Youth'. There are several yellow varieties to choose from and perhaps this at 75 cm and flowering from June until August should be selected as well as 'Butterpat', which is a similar colour but differs in being a little taller and flowering from early August until October. Both are first class and require planting at D 4–5.

Helenium 'Moerheim Beauty'. Has stood the test of time and remains one of the best and most reliable varieties. It has brown-centred large rich crimson flowers to a height of 90 cm. Flowering is from July until September. D 5.

Helenium 'Wyndley'. A compact variety to only 60 cm with a good show of large coppery orange-brown flowers from July until September. D 5.

Helichrysum

Helichrysum is only mentioned for one new and useful Perennial, recently introduced from Germany. Others are usually classed in the Shrub or Alpine plant range.

Helichrysum hybridum 'Sulphur Light' ('Schwefellicht'). Has silver-grey foliage and flowers opening sulphur-yellow on 40 cm compact bushes. These are effective from June until early September. An easy Perennial on most well-drained soils. D 4.

Heliopsis

An attractive genus sometimes known as 'Orange Sunflowers', though orange they are not! Many varieties are very similar and flower heads can be quite spectacular and up to 10 cm across. This can put a strain on the supporting stems and they sometimes flop.

However, all are reliable and long lived, requiring sun and reasonably good soil for best results.

Heliopsis 'Gigantea'. May be one of the tallest of the several varieties in cultivation but it is also one of the best, standing erectly to 120 cm. The golden-yellow flowers remain attractive from June until August. D 4.

Heliopsis 'Golden Plume'. One of the best known and finest varieties. Large double deep yellow flowers on 120 cm stems from June until September. D 4–5.

Heliopsis 'Goldgreenheart'. Somewhat dwarfer at 90 cm and has lemon-yellow double flowers tinged green at the centre from July until August. D 4–5.

Helleborus

While one of the best known perennials through Helleborus niger, *the 'Christmas Rose', there are other less demanding but equally attractive* Helleborus *species which are worthy of wider recognition. Most associate better with shrubs or in a spot on their own rather than mixed in a bed with other Perennials. Most also prefer conditions which offer some shade, good soil and a cool root run to give their best.*

Helleborus corsicus is an attractive evergreen species and not difficult to grow. It has pale apple-green flowers in February and March and large blue-green leaves normally reaching about 60 cm, but flowers and stems sometimes collapse during later summer. D 4–5.

Helleborus orientalis 'Hybrids'. There are many selected and named forms of *H. orientalis* which are very choice and rather expensive but these hybrids offer a good selection. Known as the 'Lenten Rose' *H. orientalis* 'Hybrids' come in mixed shades of pink, crimson, purple and sometimes white from January until March. Most are between 20 and 40 cm in height. D 5.

Helleborus niger. The ever-popular and often frustrating 'Christmas Rose'. Seldom in flower at Christmas it can sometimes be difficult to flower at all! It likes a good deep soil with some humus and not too dry. Young plants establish best but no rule of thumb can be followed to guarantee success. The beautiful pure white flowers on 30 cm stems are a revelation in late winter and early spring when most flowers unfurl. D 5.

Heliopsis *'Golden Plume'*.

Helleborus niger.

Hemerocallis

I cannot speak too highly of the 'Daylilies' as garden plants, for they are one of the most adaptable, reliable and hardy of any Perennials. Forming strong clumps of graceful bright green foliage they flower for weeks during mid summer – each flower lasting only a day but followed by a succession of others. In recent years in the United States and Britain there have been so many new varieties introduced that the choice becomes bewildering. I select a few well-tried yet distinctive varieties below. All will tolerate a variety of soils, wet or dry, light or heavy and succeed in full sun or some shade. Brief descriptions only are given to give space for more varieties. Flowering is mostly during June, July and August except where stated otherwise.

Hemerocallis **'Black Magic'**. Deep ruby-purple with a yellow throat. 90 cm. D 4.

Hemerocallis **'Bonanza'**. An early variety with orange flowers on 45 cm stems during July and August. D 5.

Hemerocallis **'Burning Daylight'**. An outstanding variety with large beautiful rich deep orange flowers. 90 cm. D 4.

Hemerocallis **'Golden Chimes'**. Dwarf habit producing a mass of golden-yellow flowers. 60 cm. A first-class plant. D 4.

Hemerocallis **'Hyperion'**. An old but unsurpassed clear yellow-flowered variety with beautifully scented flowers. 90 cm. D 3–4.

Hemerocallis **'Nashville'**. Large creamy flowers with a soft orange-red band. One of a newer breed of striking new introductions. 45 cm. D 4.

Hemerocallis **'Pink Damask'**. A most attractive pink variation. 75 cm. D 4.

Hemerocallis **'Stafford'**. Large-flowered bright red-yellow centre. 90 cm. D 4.

Hemerocallis **'Whichford'**. Primrose-yellow flowers of a delicate shade with a distinctive greenish centre. 45 cm. D 4.

Hemerocallis *'Bonanza'.*

Hemerocallis *'Pink Damask'.*

Hemerocallis *'Stafford'.*

Heuchera *'Bressingham Hybrids'*.　　Hosta fortunei *'Aurea'*.

Heuchera

A genus of plants which could be used more in gardens, particularly now there are some very good new varieties available, and should I say it – most raised at Bressingham since Heucheras are one of my father's specialities!

Most are easy to grow in well-drained soils but have a habit of becoming woody with age and the crowns will benefit from dividing and replanting every few years. The leaves are often attractive year round. All flower from May until July. Once again only a small selection can be made. There is a good strain of Heucheras, appropriately named 'Bressingham Hybrids', which are seed-raised and offer a pleasing show of reds, pinks, and whites.

Heuchera sanguinea **'Greenfinch'**. A plant for the flower arranger with distinctive poker-like sprays of greenish-sulphur flowers. 75 cm. D 5.

H. s. **'Hyperion'**. Similar to 'Greenfinch' but with erect spikes of deep pink flowers to 75 cm. These varieties are quite distinct in habit from the more normal Heucheras. D 5.

H. s. **'Pearl Drops'**. Whitish flowers are borne on graceful arching sprays. 60 cm. D 5.

H. s. **'Pretty Polly'**. An outstanding recent introduction. Compact clumps of green foliage form stems of 25 cm bearing dainty clear pink flowers. D 5.

H. s. **'Red Spangles'**. Free-flowering crimson-scarlet, perhaps the most popular variety. 50 cm. D 5.

H. s. **'Scintillation'**. Brilliant glistening pink flowers with reddish tips. 60 cm. D 5.

Heucherella

Heucherella *is a hybrid between the genera* Heuchera *and* Tiarella *and from this generic cross was raised one of the prettiest and choicest of Perennials.*

Heucherella **'Bridget Bloom'**, raised at Bressingham, has 45 cm spikes producing a profusion of delicate light pink flowers in May and June and often at intervals throughout the summer. It prefers light loamy soils and some shade. D 5–6.

Hosta

This genus of Hardy Perennials is also commonly known as 'The Plantain Lily'. They are fully hardy and quite adaptable, although they usually give of their best with some shade and reasonable moisture. Although grown primarily as foliage plants and as

29

such indispensable for flower arranging, some of the varieties have most attractive and sometimes sweetly scented flowers. Hostas somehow have an air of class about them and are equally suited to interplanting with shrubs as with Perennials. All become dormant in late autumn.

Hosta fortunei. Makes large dense clumps of grey-green leaves to 45 cm, above which lilac-mauve flowers give a fine show from June until August. D 3–4.

    H. f. 'Aurea'. Has beautiful golden-yellow leaves in early spring, gradually changing to light green by summer. The 60 cm flower spikes are a purplish colour during June and July. D 4.

    H. f. 'Aureomarginata'. One of the most attractive and reliable of the variegated leaved Hostas. Leaves arch outwards as they unfold in spring, deep green and edged golden yellow, reaching 60 cm. The mauve flowers on 75 cm spikes during June and July complete the picture. D 4.

    H. f. 'Picta'. Another fine form, this having pale yellow leaves in spring with a light green edge turning to light green, the margin becoming then dark green. The leaves reach 60 cm and the lilac flowers 75 cm in July and August. D 3–4.

Hosta 'Royal Standard'. An outstanding variety recently introduced from the United States. It will grow equally well in full sun or part shade where its bright green foliage is topped by 90 cm stems bearing pure white scented flowers from August until October. D 3–4.

Hosta sieboldiana 'Elegans'. A selected form of the glaucous-leaved *H. sieboldiana*. 'Elegans' produces massive clumps after several years with giant broad-ribbed grey-blue leaves to 90 cm. It creates a most magnificent effect, particularly where ample moisture is available. Unfortunately, the lilac flowers do not add much during their appearance in July and August. D 3.

Hosta 'Thomas Hogg'. A striking variegated form with large broadish green leaves margined creamy white. Mauve flowers appear on 60 cm stems during June and July. D 4. Many more worthwhile varieties exist but are too numerous to mention.

Incarvillea

Striking plants with exotic trumpet-like flowers and thick fleshy roots. They prefer a well-drained but reasonably fertile soil.

Incarvillea delavayi. The best known and most reliable form with deep pink flowers on 45 cm stems in June and July. The deeply cut green leaves offer a softer contrast to the brilliance of the flowers. D 5.

Hosta fortunei *'Aureomarginata'.*

Hosta *'Royal Standard'.*

Hosta sieboldiana *'Elegans'*.

Incarvillea delavayi.

Iris

Like some other perennial genera the Iris *are almost a subject in themselves. However, all space will allow me is a rather brief sortie into some of the most useful species and varieties.*

Iris germanica, *perhaps better known as 'The Bearded Iris' or 'Flag Iris', are popular garden plants but although often beautiful and spectacular in their short flowering period offer little for the remainder of the year. They do not to my mind, therefore, give best value for money as a border or Island Bed subject. All the same they are hardy, usually reliable and long lived, but corms or rhizomes will want dividing every few years. The best period for division and replanting is in July, directly after flowering.* I. germanica *grow happily in most soils, but require some lime and an open situation for best flowering. A very brief description of a limited selection of varieties is given below. Most flowers reach a height of between 90 and 120 cm and flower in late May and June. D 5 recommended throughout. 'Standards' refer to erect petals, 'Falls' to pendulous ones.*

Iris germanica **'Amethyst Flame'**. A beautiful blend of rosy heliotrope and light violet, ruffled pale blue beard.

I. g. **'Berkeley Gold'**. Rich yellow.

I. g. **'Black Swan'**. Almost black with a deeper beard.

I. g. **'Braithwaite'**. Lavender standards and purple falls.

I. g. **'Butterscotch Kiss'**. Can only be an American variety! Glistening caramel crinkled falls.

I. g. **'Dancer's Veil'**. Violet etching on white, ruffled falls.

I. g. **'East Indies'**. Light copper with a mauve sheen, ruffled, yellow beard.

I. g. **'Edward of Windsor'**. A clear pastel pink.

I. g. **'Frost and Flame'**. Startling snow-white with a vivid tangerine beard.

I. g. **'Party Dress'**. Ruffled peach-pink, brilliant tangerine beard.

I. g. **'Patterdale'**. An improvement on the popular old variety 'Jane Phillips' – a beautiful large pale blue.

I. g. **'Rajah'**. Orange-yellow with crimson falls.

I. g. **'Top Flight'**. Deep apricot ruffled flowers.

I. g. **'Wabash'**. An old but unsurpassed variety with white standards and violet-blue falls.

Iris pallida 'Variegata'. This and its golden variegated leaved counterpart *I. p.* 'Aurea Variegata' are first-class Perennials. Easy in sun or some shade they are primarily foliage plants with brightly variegated leaves. 'Variegata' blue-grey with white variegation. 'Aurea Variegata' with light green and golden variegation. Foliage reaches 45–50 cm and the flowers though small are a rather attractive mid blue on 60 cm spikes during June and July. D 5.

Iris pumila and varieties are rather similar to *I. germanica* but flower in April and May and are much dwarfer in habit. The flowers do not last long but are very bright when at their best. The same habit and culture applies as for the 'Bearded Iris'. All can be planted at D 7.

    I. p. 'Amber Queen'. Purple-veined white. 15 cm.

    I. p. 'Campbellii'. Bright violet-blue, a real miniature at 10 cm.

    I. p. 'Excelsa'. Light yellow. 20 cm.

Iris sibirica and its varieties are unspectacular but most useful as waterside plants, although equally adaptable to almost any soil. All have rush-like leaves and a clump-forming habit. During June and July small flowers appear on 75–90 cm spikes and flower briefly. D 4 would apply for all.

    I. s. 'Ottawa'. Deep blue flowers, flecked white.

    I. s. 'Perry's Blue'. A larger flower than most, sky-blue.

    I. s. 'Snow Queen'. Ivory-white.

    I. s. 'Tropic Night'. Dark purple.

Iris stylosa, also often listed under the almost unpronounceable name of *I. unguicularis*, is the only winter-flowering *Iris* and certainly one of the few Perennials flowering from January until March. Clumps of rushy leaves produce lavender-blue flowers nestling on 30 cm stems close to the foliage. A sunny dry position gives the best chance of annual flower.

Iris *'Braithwaite'*. Iris *'Frost and Flame'*. Iris *'Patterdale'*.

Iris *'Rajah'*. Iris pumila *'Campbellii'*.

Kniphofia *'Samuel's Sensation'*.   Kniphofia *'Shining Sceptre'*.

Kniphofia

The common name 'Red Hot Poker' is an apt one as far as it goes. The fact is that there is now a tremendous range of varieties in shades of red, orange, yellow and white and almost any colour in between. They are some of the most spectacular and useful of Perennials, usually long lived and associating well with Shrubs as well as among other Hardy Perennials and particularly Ornamental Grasses.

Culturally they require a well-drained position in sun or part shade and dislike winter wet. Division should be made in spring. It is a useful practice in cold districts to tie the rushy leaves together in late autumn to prevent snow or wet penetrating to the crowns where it can freeze and cause damage. Most when established are perfectly hardy except in winters of extreme severity. Some of the most distinct and reliable varieties are listed below.

Kniphofia **'Atlanta'**. a large glaucous-leaved variety with massive spikes of yellow and red flowers reaching 90 cm and flowering during June and July. D 3.

Kniphofia galpinii. This dwarf species is a beautiful late-flowering poker but somewhat unreliable in cold districts and on poorly drained soils, and the species itself is seldom offered. However, some first-class varieties have been raised in recent years which largely overcome these faults.

K. g. **'Bressingham Comet'**. An outstanding new variety with the typical *galpinii* grassy leaves with 50 cm spikes of brilliant orange tipped red through September and October. D 5.

K. g. **'Bressingham Flame'**. This is another selection which flowers much earlier, from July and lasting until September. The 75 cm flowers spikes are numerous and a deep orange flame. D 4.

Kniphofia **'Jenny Bloom'**. An unusual colour, long 90 cm spikes have flowers of salmon-pink overlaying a peach shade. Flowering period is July and August. D 4–5.

Kniphofia **'Little Maid'**. A superb recent introduction, reliable, floriferous and dwarf. Barely 60 cm high it has creamy yellow tipped flower spikes fading to ivory from August until October. D 4.

33

Kniphofia 'Royal Standard'. One of the oldest and most reliable varieties with 90 cm red and yellow spikes from June until August. D 4.

Kniphofia 'Samuel's Sensation'. A most striking selection with tall 150 cm spikes of scarlet during August and September. D 3–4.

Kniphofia 'Shining Sceptre'. A new variety with large flower heads of clear yellow shading to primrose-ivory on sturdy 100 cm spikes. Flowers in July and August. A distinct newcomer. D 5.

Lamium

This 'Dead Nettle' genus are not really suitable for the perennial border or Island Bed but among them are some excellent ground coverers tolerating dry, sunny banks as well as root impoverished shady areas as well as any plants, though most are apt to become invasive on moist or rich soils.

Lamium galeobdolon 'Variegatum'. One of the best ground-cover plants for banks or under trees, where it quickly forms a carpet of light green and silver variegated leaves. The yellow flowers appear in May and June over 20 cm high foliage. D 4.

Lamium maculatum 'Chequers'. This, the most distinctive form of *L. maculatum*, is much more compact and mat-forming in growth than the more rampant *L. g.* 'Variegatum'. It has dark green leaves with an attractive central silvery-white stripe. The deep pink flowers open in April and last through May on 30 cm stems. D 3.

Summer in the Dell Garden. Yucca filamentosa *(right foreground) makes an excellent foil against* Kniphofia *'Bressingham Flame' (centre) and beyond* Agapanthus patens *(centre right).*

Liatris callilepis 'Kobold'.

Ligularia stenocephala 'The Rocket'.

Liatris

Generally reliable and trouble-free Perennials which grow from a fleshy tuberous root and are remarkable for their unusual habit of throwing up spikes which on flowering open from the top first. Although not really fussy they prefer lighter, reasonably well-drained soils. Their showy purple spikes are excellent for cutting.

Liatris callilepis. The best known 'Gayfeather', with rigid spikes reaching 90 cm and fluffy 'bottlebrush' lilac-purple flowers from July until September. D 5.

L. c. 'Kobold'. An excellent dwarf variety with intense deep lilac flowers on sturdy 60 cm spikes from July to September. D 5–6.

Ligularia

These large-growing plants require moist conditions to support their abundant foliage and large flowers, although preferring sun to shade. There are many species and varieties which make ideal waterside subjects or they can be used in gardens where ample space is available.

Ligularia clivorum 'Desdemona'. Has large handsome purplish leaves contrasting well with bright orange-yellow flowers on branching 120 cm spikes. The flowering period lasts from July until September. D 3.

Ligularia stenocephala 'The Rocket'. This selected form, with large deeply cut leaves of deep green and imposing 150 cm black-stemmed spikes, bears bright yellow flowers in July and August. A most striking Perennial for moisture or waterside. D 4.

Liriope

A group of plants which have yet to make their mark in Britain, being used much more widely in the United States. Hardy and tolerating both full sun or shade, they are most charming and useful late-blooming Perennials. All varieties have evergreen foliage and prefer lighter well-drained soils.

Liriope muscari. Is the best and grows in grassy hummocks from which emerge short 30 cm spikes of bright violet-purple, lasting from August until October. D 5.

Lupinus

Long one of the most popular of Perennials, 'Lupins' still can provide one of the brightest spots in any garden when in full flower. Unfortunately, there can be drawbacks – they do not live long in limy, chalky soils and some of the named varieties, magnificent colours though they are, have succumbed to disease and are not always reliable even if they can be obtained. Lupins prefer light soils with a neutral or acid pH and will live much longer given these conditions.

All of the old named favourites have to be propagated by cuttings and if you can get them are likely to be more expensive than seed-raised varieties, many of which now come true to colour. All flower in June and July, and cutting back the flower stalks after flowering will prevent a crop of self-sown seedlings which are mostly inferior in colour. Seed or plants of 'Russell Hybrids' to my mind is the most rewarding way to have a splash of colour in your garden with little effort – these having usually been selected from only the best plants give real value for money. D 3. No recommended list of varieties is given bearing the above comments in mind.

Lychnis

Although there are several species and varieties of the 'Campions' a great many are classed as Alpines and others are not reliably perennial. However, those mentioned below are certain to give a good account of themselves given conditions which they like.

Lychnis chalcedonica. A striking Perennial of easy cultivation with vivid scarlet flowers on flattish heads in June and July. These are borne on 90 cm stems, although in dry conditions somewhat less. D 5.

Lychnis coronaria **'Atrosanguinea'**. Although not long lived is easily raised from seed and produces mounds of silver leaves against which the bright magenta flowers make a fine contrast from June until September. Good drainage is essential for best results. Height 60 cm. D 5.

Lychnis viscaria **'Splendens Plena'**. A good front of the border plant with short grassy green leaves and 30 cm wiry sprays carrying large double cerise flowers from June until July. Again sun and a well-drained soil will give longevity. D 5–6.

Lysimachia

The 'Loosestrifes', if not actually requiring waterside conditions, dislike dry soils but otherwise are quite trouble free.

Lysimachia clethroides. A clump-forming species with 90 cm spikes of green

Lysimachia punctata.　　　　　　　　　Lupin *Russell Hybrids.*

Lythrum salicaria *'Firecandle'*.

Meconopsis betonicifolia.

terminating in arching heads of charming white flowers during August and September. D 4–5.

Lysimachia punctata. The 'Yellow Loosestrife' is an easy and showy Perennial with whorls of bright yellow flowers against fresh green foliage from June until August. The height will vary from 80–100 cm according to the amount of moisture available. Apt to be a trifle invasive. D 4.

Lythrum

A limited yet popular genus, the 'Purple Loosestrife' could lay claims to being one of the hardiest and most adaptable of Perennials. Preferring moisture, they will succeed in almost any soils with their tough woody roots and erect sturdy stems bearing shades of pink, red and purple flowers. All varieties flower during the July to September period.

Lythrum salicaria **'Firecandle'** ('Feuerkerze'). Probably the brightest variety, with intense rosy-red flowers on 90 cm spikes. D 4–5.

 L. s. **'Robert'.** Has a more bushy habit than 'Firecandle' and bright pink flowers. The height is only 60–75 cm. D 5.

Lythrum virgatum **'The Rocket'.** This variety has the more erect habit of this species with 90 cm spikes of deep rosy red. D 4.

Meconopsis betonicifolia (baileyi)

Should not perhaps be included in this booklet although it is probably the most reliably perennial of these 'Blue Poppies'. It is, however, quite a choice plant for those who have the right conditions – moist, humus-rich soils and part shade – and like a challenge. The sight of the clear glacier-like blue flowers in May and June is reward enough even though this famous 'Himalayan Poppy' tends to flower itself to death within a few seasons. Plants can be purchased or else seed saved to make up for any losses. D 5.

Top: Oenothera missouriensis.
Bottom: Monarda didyma *'Cambridge Scarlet'.*

Top: Nepeta faassenii.
Bottom: Oenothera tetragona *'Highlight'.*

Monarda

Generally reliable and showy plants with curiously shaped flowers and aromatic foliage being some of the most popular of Hardy Perennials. Most varieties are quite vigorous and mat forming, throwing up masses of bright flowers during mid to late summer. If the tendency of the plant is to wander out from the centre it can easily be curbed and the more vigorous outside pieces replanted back in the middle of the group. March is the best time for this. Some moisture is preferred but Monardas will grow happily in most garden soils. All grow to about 90 cm.

***Monarda didyma* 'Cambridge Scarlet'.** Though an old variety is still unbeatable for its brilliant scarlet flowers which last from July until September. D 4.

***M. d.* 'Croftway Pink'.** Bright rose-pink flowers start in June and last until September. D 4.

***M. d.* 'Prairie Night'.** Most effective with deep violet-purple heads and dark green foliage if planted against some contrasting Perennial such as a *Solidago.* Flowering period from June until September. D 4.

***M. d.* 'Snow Maiden'.** The only white, which is unfortunately not a particularly strong flower but quite distinctive, flowering from June until September. D 5.

Nepeta faassenii (mussinii)

This is not the only 'Catmint' but probably the most useful and certainly the best known. Not reliably long lived but producing a marvellous show of light violet-blue flowers on and off from May until September, and with its grey leaves makes an attractive edging plant. Requiring well-drained soil, it will withstand the driest of conditions but it is much better in sun than shade. Trim back flowering spikes in March or early April to produce more compact basal growth. Height 30 cm. D 5.

Nerine bowdenii

A bulb which fits in well with Perennials or shrubs or as an individual feature against a south wall. Strap-like leaves appear in spring then die away in late summer. This is only a preparation for the beautiful trumpet flowers which appear on 45 cm stems in October and last until December. Once established it is practically hardy in most of the British Isles but prefers a well-drained soil and a sunny situation. In cold areas it will pay to protect with bracken or leaves through the winter. D 7.

Oenothera

Generally known as the 'Evening Primrose' this genus has some charming species and varieties – all with yellow flowers. Not difficult but they will succeed best on loamy soil which has good drainage and does not dry out. Sun preferred. Propagation of rosette types is by division in spring, while missouriensis *is raised from seed.*

Oenothera **'Fireworks'** ('Fyrverkeri'). One of the rosette-forming varieties which are shallow rooted, and it is these types which resent drought the most. Purple-green foliage produces 45 cm flowering stems with red buds which open to bright yellow flowers lasting on and off from June until August. D 5.

Oenothera missouriensis (syn. macrocarpa). One of the best of all Perennials, with large cup-shaped flowers of pure yellow on prostrate leafy stems, produced in succession from June until September. Because long fleshy roots are able to withstand prolonged drought this is an ideal plant for sunny banks or front of the border positions. Height 25 cm. D 5.

Oenothera tetragona **'Highlight'** ('Hohes Licht'). Of German origin, this is perhaps the brightest and most floriferous of all Oenotheras. Attractive shiny bluish-green leaves in spring are followed by large yellow flowers on 60 cm stems from June until September. D 5.

Omphalodes

A small genus of plants with 'Forget-me-not' flowers which prefer some shade.

Omphalodes cappadocica **'Anthea Bloom'**. An improved form making leafy 15 cm hummocks and masses of intense sky-blue flowers from April until early June. Where some shade and reasonable moisture are available this makes a marvellous spring show. D 5.

Origanum

The two members of this 'Marjoram' genus mentioned below are useful Perennials though little known. Both prefer sun and good drainage and are easy growers.

Origanum laevigatum. Dark blue-green leaves, wiry erect 40 cm stems with small purple flowers creating a hazy effect when in flower from July until September. D 5.

Origanum vulgare **'Aureum'**. Is the golden-leaved form of the 'Common Marjoram' and prefers a sunny situation where it forms 25 cm high clumps of aromatic foliage. The flowers are almost non-existent but this foliage plant is good in association with contrasting Perennials. D 5.

Pachysandra terminalis

One of the best ground covers for shade and under trees. It has a slow spreading habit with bright green deeply lobed leaves 15–20 cm high. The rather insignificant whitish flowers are produced in February and March. There is an attractive variegated form with silvery-white and green leaves, if anything slightly dwarfer and slower growing than the type. Not plants to be considered for an Island Bed but most useful in places where little else will grow. D 5.

Paeonia 'P. Roosevelt'.   Paeonia 'Sarah Bernhardt'.   Paeonia lobata 'Sunshine'.

Paeonia

The 'Paeony' has won for itself a place of distinction among Hardy Perennials partly because of its reputation for being long lived but mostly because of its often spectacular flowers. Generally adaptable to most soils they usually prefer good drainage and a fair share of sun.

Paeonias should be planted before March in order to establish a fresh root system before pushing up their new season's growth. The young shoots require planting an inch or two below ground level and care must be taken during this operation not to snap off brittle roots. Good deep soil enriched by compost or manure will get plants off to a good start, and top dressing with fertilised humus every two or three years will increase flowering capacity. Flowering from small plants is unlikely for at least the first year after planting so one should look for a reasonable sized plant and early planting if immediate results are required! Early autumn is the best time for division and this should be done with care. Brief descriptions are given of only a few selected varieties of the lactiflora types – the popular 'June flowering' Paeonies. All except 'Bowl of Beauty' have double flowers and are between 75 and 90 cm in height.

Paeonia 'Bowl of Beauty'. Though a single-flowered variety is a magnificent Paeony which has enormous rose-cupped flowers with a cream centre. Also June flowering and growing to 90 cm or thereabouts. D 3.

Paeonia lactiflora 'Cherry Hill'. Bright cherry-red. D 3.

   P. l. 'Duchesse de Nemours'. Cream turning to white, scented. D 3.

   P. l. 'Edulis Superba'. Bright rose-pink, scented. D 3.

   P. l. 'Felix Crousse'. Striking carmine-red. D 3.

   P. l. 'Festiva Maxima'. Large flowered white, flecked crimson. D 3.

   P. l. 'Karl Rosenfield'. Deep crimson. D 3.

   P. l. 'President Roosevelt'. Deep red. D 3.

   P. l. 'Sarah Bernhardt'. Always popular. Large apple-blossom pink flowers. D 3.

   P. l. 'Solange'. Salmon-rose paling towards the centre. D 3.

Paeonia lobata (peregrina) 'Sunshine'. This single-flowered variety is a choice and not very often seen Paeony. It has brilliant salmon flowers in May and June on 75 cm stems. D 4.

Paeonia mlokosewitchii Has an almost unpronounceable name but is a beautifully delicate-looking plant with single yellow cup-shaped flowers in late April and May. Not a difficult plant to grow although classed as choice. Height 60 cm. D 3–4.

Paeonia officinalis. Varieties of this species are commonly classed as 'Old Cottage

Garden Paeonies', flowering mostly in May and generally being less demanding in their requirements than the June flowering types. 'Alba Plena', 'Rosea Plena' and 'Rubra Plena' with their large frilled heads of double white, rose and red flowers are to my mind equally attractive. D 3.

Papaver orientalis

The 'Oriental Poppies', though not trouble free as border plants, have flowers unrivalled for brilliance even if some could almost be described as gaudy! All have long hairy leaves and large vividly coloured flowers which often cannot be supported by their stems without staking. Sun and good drainage are important ingredients for success and longevity. Cut back foliage after flowering.

Papaver orientalis 'Goliath'. Has proved itself one of the best and most reliable varieties, and holds its large crimson-scarlet flowers erectly on 90 cm stems without staking during May and June. A first-class Perennial which draws the eye to its brilliance. D 4.

P. o. 'Marcus Perry'. Large orange-scarlet flower heads, borne on sturdy 75 cm stems, are almost 15 cm across. Flowering period is from May until July. D 4.

P. o. 'Mrs Perry'. Introduced over seventy years ago and still going strong! Dark blotched salmon-pink flower heads are borne on 90 cm stems from May to July. D 4.

P. o. 'Perry's White'. Of similar height to 'Mrs Perry', with white flowers and dark blotches, this makes a good show through late May, June and July. D 4.

P. o. 'Turkish Delight'. Has large heads of glistening pink on 90 cm stems in May and June. D 5.

Phlox

Most of those mentioned below are the paniculata (decussata) *types which are among the best known and, with reason, among the most popular of Hardy Perennials. The multitudes of varieties which have been introduced over the years have given a wide range of colours, and the list below, of course, can only give what I would regard as the most reliable and distinct. Now to cultivation:* Phlox paniculata *and varieties prefer a fertile loamy or sandy soil which retains some moisture during dry periods, and sun or part shade. Plants have long fibrous roots which should be planted to their full depth in humus-enriched soil. Mulching with compost every other year will maintain healthy growth and flowering, but at least every four to five years replanting may be necessary for rejuvenation. The best way to do this is to slice off the top of an old plant 5 cm below ground in late winter and dig up the subsequent young plants which will sprout in May from the roots left behind. These can then be replanted, first having*

Papaver orientalis *'Goliath'.*   Phlox paniculata *'Pinafore Pink'.*

prepared and composted the old area. Propagation from division or tip cuttings is not recommended due to the susceptibility of Phlox to eelworm.

All the Phlox paniculata varieties briefly described below bear fragrant flower trusses during the July to early October period. Heights are given in figures after each description. D 4–5.

***Phlox paniculata* 'Brigadier'.** Glowing salmon-scarlet. 100 cm.

P. p. **'Chintz'.** Warm pink with a red eye. 75 cm.

P. p. **'Fairy's Petticoat'.** Pale mauve with a darker eye. Strong growing. 90 cm.

P. p. **'Gaiety'.** Bright cherry-red suffused orange. 75 cm.

P. p. **'Hampton Court'.** Helio-blue with dark foliage. 75 cm.

P. p. **'Harlequin'.** Rich purple flowers, dark green and creamy-white variegated leaves. A striking plant. 90 cm.

P. p. **'Marlborough'.** Purple flowers on compact bushes. 75 cm.

P. p. **'Mother of Pearl'.** White delicately suffused pink. 75 cm.

P. p. **'Mount Fujiyama'.** Erect habit, large pure white heads. 90 cm.

P. p. **'Pinafore Pink'.** Dwarf bushy habit, large heads of clear bright pink. 60 cm.

P. p. **'Prince of Orange'.** Outstanding brilliant orange-salmon flowers, good habit. 90 cm.

P. p. **'Prospero'.** Pale lilac. 90 cm.

P. p. **'Red Indian'.** Vivid deep-crimson flowers. 90 cm.

P. p. **'Sandringham'.** Cyclamen-pink, darker centre, always popular. 75 cm.

P. p. **'Starfire'.** Dark leaves and the brightest red of any Phlox. Vigorous, healthy growth. 90 cm.

P. p. **'Vintage Wine'.** Large heads of purple-red. 75 cm.

P. p. **'White Admiral'.** The most popular and reliable white. 90 cm.

Phlox paniculata *'White Admiral'.*

Above: Phlox paniculata *'Red Indian'.*
Below: Phlox paniculata *'Prince of Orange'.*

Platycodon grandiflorum 'Mariesii'.

Physostegia virginiana 'Vivid'.

Physalis franchettii

Although the 'Cape Gooseberry' or 'Chinese Lantern', as it is known, is not a good border plant it is an extremely attractive and deservedly popular Perennial. While its vigorous habit and running roots can cause problems to other less invasive plants, in a spot of its own it is little trouble and is always rewarding in late autumn and winter. The lush green leaves of summer slowly wither in autumn to exhibit large orange-red fruit bags in among the foliage. These dry well and are invaluable for winter decoration. It grows to 75 cm, the lanterns remaining effective outdoors from September until December. D 4.

Physostegia

A small yet distinctive genus with the unusual common name of the 'Obedient Plant'. This relates to the flowers on the spikes which remain where put when moved aside with the finger instead of springing back or breaking. All varieties have roots which run below ground and, though not difficult to control, may need curbing and planting back in the middle of the group. Sun and reasonably moist soils seem to provide the best results.

Physostegia virginiana 'Summer Snow'. Has 75 cm spikes with pretty tubular-lipped pure white flowers lasting from July until September. D 4–5.

P. v. 'Summer Spire'. The counterpart to the previous variety is of a similar height and habit but has rose-pink flowers on slender tapering spikes. Flowering period is if anything earlier than 'Summer Snow'. D 4.

P. v. 'Vivid'. Definitely the variety for the smaller border or the modern smaller garden though not flowering until August. The rigid 60 cm spikes carry brilliant rose-coloured flowers until as late as November – a most useful Perennial. D 4.

Platycodon

Though often commonly known as the 'Balloon Flower' because of its habit of forming little bags of petals before opening, the other common name 'Chinese' or 'Japanese Bellflower' is more descriptive of the opened flowers, which closely resemble the related Campanulas. These are trouble-free plants with fleshy roots which will grow well in any well-drained soil.

Platycodon grandiflorum 'Mariesii'. A first-class dwarf variety to only 45 cm. The stems terminate in beautiful azure-blue veined flowers from July until September. Being seed-raised some variation in blue shades may occur. D 5–6.

***P. g.* 'Snowflake'.** Is outstanding with pure white semi-double flowers on 60 cm stems held much more erectly than 'Mariesii' and providing a bright spot in any border during July and August. D 5–6.

Polemonium

A favourite old 'Cottage Garden Plant', the 'Jacob's Ladder' is still a good though little-used plant these days, although good garden varieties have been introduced in recent years superseding the short-lived and self-seeding Polemonium. The two varieties mentioned below are easy Perennials for sun or part shade.

***Polemonium* 'Blue Pearl'.** The dwarfest variety, growing to only 25 cm with short spikes of blue flowers in May and June. D 5.

Polemonium foliosissimum. Without doubt the most impressive 'Jacob's Ladder', with dense fresh green leafy growth producing 75 cm stems bearing clusters of lavender-blue flowers. —These last over a long period – from May until August – and have the added advantage of not seeding themselves all over the garden when finished. D 5.

Polygonum

This genus has an undeserved reputation based upon a few large-growing and invasive species which certainly are not suitable as garden plants. Those mentioned below are unquestionably attractive and useful Perennials whose main requirement is adequate moisture. Some are clump forming, some have shallow-rooting surface growth, and these latter types will withstand both dry shade and hot sun.

***Polygonum affine* 'Darjeeling Red'.** Possibly the best for ground cover, an improvement upon the type by its larger-headed yet shorter flowering spikes. These rise to 25 cm above a carpet of narrow green leaves from June until September and are deep rose-pink. Even when flowering has finished, the dead heads remain attractive. There is an excellent though slightly less reliable variety, 'Donald Lowndes', with more compact foliage and shorter flower stems. These produce rose-pink spikes from early June onwards, turning a beautiful russet colour during early and late autumn. Not so adaptable as ground cover. D 4–5.

***Polygonum bistorta* 'Superbum'.** An easy no-nonsense plant which will grow under almost any conditions where not too dry, and is excellent as a waterside subject. Leafy mats produce large pink bottle-brush flowers on 90 cm stems on and off from May until August. D 3–4.

Polygonum milettii. Is quite a choice plant, which needs moisture. From small clumps of dark green leaves appear poker-like 45 cm spikes of deepest red flowering continuously from June until September. D 6.

Polygonum bistorta *'Superbum'.*　　　　Potentilla *'Glory of Nancy'*

Primula sieboldii *'Snowflakes'*.
Primula rosea *'Delight'*.

Potentilla

The herbaceous side of this large genus offer a generally wider range of colours than the shrubby types and are among the most useful and trouble free of Perennials. Most varieties are 45 cm or less in height and flower for long periods in the summer. Sun and good drainage again preferred. Only a few distinct varieties can be described here, while the smaller-growing sorts can be found described under Alpines.

***Potentilla atrosanguinea* 'Gibson's Scarlet'.** Is certainly the most popular variety and one of the best of all perennial garden plants. Brilliant scarlet-red single flowers open in June and continue until August and are offset by the pleasant fresh green of the strawberry-like leaves. Height 30 cm. D 5.

P. a. **'Glory of Nancy'.** Has grey-green foliage, a more erect habit to 45 cm and large semi-double flowers of orange-crimson creating a striking effect in any border from June until August. D 4–5.

***Potentilla* 'Wm. Rollison'.** One of the brightest and most reliable of varieties with nearly double dazzling bright orange-flame flowers to 40 cm during the June to August period. D 5.

***Potentilla* 'Yellow Queen'.** This variety, though not new, deserves to be better known. It has silvery-green foliage and clear yellow semi-double flowers only 30 cm high, lasting from June until August. D 5.

Primula

A large and extremely diverse genus, most of which unfortunately need special conditions to succeed and others which are relatively short lived. However, for those who are lucky enough to have woodland or moisture conditions Primulas offer a wide choice. But since they are rather a large and specialist subject I propose to mention only a few that could be regarded as reliable Hardy Perennials.

Primula denticulata. With its 'drumstick' heads in shades of lilac, or light lilac-blue is probably one of the best known and easiest of Primulas to grow. Requiring moist soil, its flowers reach 30 cm in height and last from March until May. There are some selected forms of *denticulata* in 'Alba', a very showy form with pure white flowers, and 'Rubin', which has beautiful heads of ruby-red. Both have similar heights and flowering times to the species. All are D 5.

***Primula rosea* 'Delight'.** Pushes its flower buds above ground in early March, opening to the most brilliant cerise-red flowers, then fading to a deep pink. These flowers reach only 10–15 cm and last into May. Moisture is essential for success in growing this plant. D 6–7.

Primula sieboldii. Perhaps these types should be more in an alpine plant category but again will require special situations in which to endure. All are clump forming, with slightly hairy soft green leaves and need cool moist soil with some shade.

***P. s.* 'Geisha Girl'.** Deep pink flowers are held on loose 15 cm trusses in April and May. D 6–7.

***P. s.* 'Snowflakes'.** An outstanding plant with dazzling white flowers in April and May. D 6–7.

Prunella

An easy-growing genus of mat-forming habit and short spikes of lipped tubular flowers, mostly from the June to August period. Adaptable to sun or some shade, useful for ground cover and trouble free.

***Prunella webbiana* 'Little Red Riding Hood'** ('Rotkappchen'). A relatively recent introduction which is a distinct improvement over some old varieties. Dwarf 15 cm spikes are covered in rosy-maroon coloured flowers. D 5–6.

***Prunella webbiana* 'Loveliness'.** Has sturdy 25 cm spikes of lilac flowers. D 5.

***P. w.* 'Loveliness Pink'.** From the same stable, so to speak, has clear pink flowers on 30 cm spikes. D 5.

***P. w.* 'Loveliness White'.** Completes the colour range. An attractive form. 25 cm spikes. D 5.

Pulmonaria

These are easy spring-flowering subjects with few faults. Adaptable to sun or shade, their only dislike is for extremely dry situations. All have a spreading clumpy habit useful as ground coverers, with quite large hairy leaves, some varieties being prettily spotted or mottled. Flowers are bell shaped and held on short sprays between 20 and 30 cm. in height, lasting from March until May.

***Pulmonaria angustifolia* 'Azurea'.** The brightest of the blue varieties, with azure flower sprays. D 4–5.

***Pulmonaria saccharata* 'Bowles Red'.** Has a vigorous habit creating leafy mats of fresh green foliage, and small bright red flower sprays. D 4.

***P. s.* 'Pink Dawn'.** The sprays of pinkish flowers in spring are enhanced by striking leaves which are green, spotted silvery white. D 4–5.

Pyrethrum

Like so many other 'standard' and once popular Perennials the Pyrethrums have lost vigour and reliability and perhaps consequently popularity in recent years. They are not, in a word, 'in fashion' although in my view they still have few equals as cut flowers. They require a well-drained soil and an open situation but even so most varieties will need staking to prevent stem collapse. All are clump forming with fibrous

Pulmonaria *'Pink Dawn'*.   Pyrethrum *'Bressingham Red'*.

roots and carroty foliage producing flowers on 60–90 cm stems from late May until early July. Spring division and planting is advisable.

A very limited recommended list is made below from the innumerable varieties which have been introduced over the years. The doubles are usually less vigorous.

Single flowered. Mostly from 70 to 90 cm in height. D 4.
  'Avalanche': White. 'Brenda': Deep cerise-pink. 'Bressingham Red': Reliable and showy. 'Eileen May Robinson': Perhaps the most popular of all. Large salmon-pink. 'Evenglow': Dwarfer, good habit, salmon-red. 'Kelway's Glorious': An old favourite crimson-scarlet.

Double flowered. Mostly 60–70 cm in height. D 5.
  'Lord Rosebery': Deep crimson. 'Madeleine': A fine light pink. 'Prospero': Warm salmon-pink. 'Princess de Laeken': Outstanding carmine-red. 'Vanessa': Beautiful deep pink raised at Bressingham. 'White Madeleine': The most reliable white.

The flint summerhouse, naturally set among Perennials, is a focal point of the Dell Garden.

Ranunculus

Most people have the mistaken impression that all the 'Buttercup' family are weedy. There are, however, some quite choice varieties and others which are useful border plants, though little known. Most prefer soil which does not dry out.

***Ranunculus aconitifolius* 'Plenus'.** A choice plant requiring moisture to produce a marvellous show of snow-white double-button flowers on 45 cm stems from May until July. D 5.

***Ranunculus bulbosus* 'Speciosus Plenus'.** This somewhat cumbersome name hides an attractive dwarf 'Buttercup' with large double yellow-green centred flowers. Growing to 25 cm in height and flowering from May until July, it is not the least invasive and requires merely moist conditions. D 5.

Ranunculus gramineus. Does not have any special requirements beyond a reasonable garden soil and will grow well either in sun or part shade. It has glaucous grassy leaves and shining yellow flowers on 30 cm stems from May until July. D 6.

Rodgersia pinnata 'Superba'. Rudbeckia fulgida 'Goldsturm'.

Rodgersia

These extremely ornamental plants are attractive for their leaves as much as for their flowers. Moisture is a definite requirement, shade less so, to provide the abundant growth these plants make. They respond to a mulching of compost in spring and if treated well will live many years undisturbed.

Rodgersia pinnata. A superb form with handsome deeply fingered chestnut-like leaves and panicles of creamy-white scented flowers on erect 90 cm stems. These flowers usually last through July and August. D 3–4.

    R. p. 'Superba'. A magnificent plant with bronzy-purple chestnut leaves and deep rose flowers during June, July and August. Height 90 cm. D 3–4.

Rodgersia tabularis. Has distinctive flat umbrella-like fresh leaves, providing a canopy of apple-green some 60 cm high, above which rise creamy Astilbe-type flowers to 80 cm. Flowering is generally in June and July. D 4.

Rudbeckia

Among these 'Cone Flowers' are some varieties which to my mind are indispensable to the perennial border. Most are easy growers on all but the driest of soils and prefer a sunny situation. Some of the taller varieties are not suitable except for large gardens and even there they will need staking, so I have restricted the choice to three of the dwarfer types.

Rudbeckia fulgida 'deamii'. One of the 'Black-Eyed Susan' types with deep yellow petals and a dark cone-like centre. It grows erectly to 90 cm, producing a marvellous show of flowers from July until October. D 5.

Rudbeckia f. 'Goldsturm'. One of my favourites, with masses of deep golden-yellow flowers contrasting with the black central cone from July until October. Of compact habit it reaches only 75 cm, hardy and trouble free. D 5.

Rudbeckia laciniata 'Goldquelle'. An outstanding plant of bushy habit with bright green foliage and large double deep yellow flowers to 90 cm, lasting from August until October. D 4–5.

Salvia

The diverse and numerous 'Sages' include some very good Hardy Perennials. Most of those described below require a reasonably open situation with good drainage.

Salvia argentea. A striking foliage plant with large silver-grey hairy leaves and 75 cm spikes of white flowers during July and August. A sunny well-drained situation is required for best results. D 4.

Salvia haematodes. An attractive plant with branched 90 cm spikes bearing light lilac-blue flowers from June until August. D 5.

S. h. 'Indigo'. This cross with *S. superba* has produced a striking plant with deep blue flowers on 100 cm spikes. These last from June until August, adding an 'architectural' character to the border. D 5.

Salvia nemerosa 'May Night' ('Mainacht'). Makes a fine show of rich violet-blue flowers from May until September – a feat not equalled by many other Perennials. Growing to only 45 cm it is very effective in a mass at the front of the border. A first-rate introduction. D 5.

S. n. 'Superba'. Has long been a popular Perennial and with good reason. Compact leafy bushes produce masses of violet-purple flowers on 90 cm spikes from July until September. The purple haze of flowers in late summer make a good combination planted with *Rudbeckia f.* 'deamii' or 'Goldsturm'. D 4–5.

S. n. 'East Friesland'. Is worth mentioning as a dwarf form of 'Superba' with similar attributes but reaching only 45 cm and is therefore better suited to the small garden. D 5.

Salvia nemerosa *'May Night' stands out in the foreground of this Bressingham border.*

Scabiosa

Some of these varieties of S. Caucasica *have proved unreliable, leaving the more robust 'Clive Greaves' the undisputed favourite. The secret even with this, the most reliable variety, is to keep it young, since old plants lose vigour and young healthy pieces with fibrous roots are required for successful rejuvenation. Spring is without doubt the best time for division and replanting, and old woody stems and roots should be discarded. Light loamy preferably limy soils with good drainage will provide best results. All are excellent for cutting over a long period.*

***Scabiosa caucasica* 'Bressingham White'.** Can be recommended as probably the strongest growing white variety – all whites being somewhat less vigorous than the blues – with fresh green deeply cut foliage and large flat-headed flowers on 75 cm stems. Flowering usually begins in June and lasts on and off until September. D 5.

S. c. 'Clive Greaves'. Must be one of the most popular Perennials of all time. It has large rich blue flower heads on 75 cm stems which bloom continuously from June until September. Marvellous as a cut flower. D 5.

Scabiosa graminifolia. A different type, almost sub-shrubby in appearance with compact 25 cm bushes of narrow silvery-grey leaves. Smallish mauve pincushion-like flowers are borne in succession from June until September. D 5.

S. g. 'Pinkushion'. A pink form of the above with similar attributes. Both are excellent front of the border subjects, long lived and trouble free. D 5.

Schizostylis

Though perhaps not fully hardy in cold exposed parts of Britain the 'Kaffir Lily' and its varieties are among the most striking of autumn-flowering Perennials. In a sheltered spot with sun or part shade and good drainage, though not too dry they will quickly establish by underground rhizomes and be reliably perennial. The rhizomes become congested after three or four years and may need thinning, otherwise flowering may deteriorate. Spring division, mulching, and planting is recommended.

***Schizostylis coccinea* 'Major'.** The strongest and brightest form, with 75 cm spikes bearing large red gladioli-like flowers during October and November. D 5.

S. c. 'November Cheer'. A recently introduced variety with glistening pink flowers on 75 cm stems in October and November. D 5.

Scabiosa caucasica *'Clive Greaves'.*  Schizostylis coccinea *'Major'.*

Sedum spectabile 'Autumn Joy'.　　　　　Sidalcea 'Loveliness'.

Sedum

The 'Stonecrop' family consists of a wide range of species and varieties, most of which are classed as Alpines but some are invaluable Hardy Perennial subjects. Most of these are of easy culture, requiring mainly sun and reasonable drainage for success, and little aftercare. Most have succulent-type leaves and are attractive both as foliage and flowering plants.

Sedum rhodiola. (syn. rosea). A curiously attractive *Sedum* with a clumpy fleshy root. In spring shoots of short glaucous leaves push their way up to a height of 25 cm, terminating in yellow flower heads. A neat and unusual plant for a frontal position. D 5.
Sedum spectabile. Known as the 'Iceplant', this and its varieties are first-rate dwarf Hardy Perennials. This species is an attractive plant with greyish-white succulent foliage and large flat heads of light pink flowers from August until October. Height 35 cm. D 5.
　S. s. 'Autumn Joy'. Must be among the top ten Perennials. Attractive from spring onwards when fleshy grey-green foliage appears, to be followed by 40 cm high heads of salmon-pink flowers in August. These gradually turn reddish bronze in October, dying down as winter sets in. D 4.

Sidalcea

Reliable and beautiful plants which should have a place in most perennial borders or beds. Again like so many Perennials sun and good drainage is preferred and in these conditions these 'Mallows' will give continued satisfaction. All have a clump-forming habit with attractively cut fresh green leaves from which grow sturdy leafy spikes. These vary in height but flower mostly in June and July and sometimes to August.

Sidalcea 'Croftway Red'. A robust variety with 90 cm spikes of rich deep red. D 5.
Sidalcea 'Loveliness'. Dwarf and compact habit with lovely clear shell-pink flowers on 75 cm stems. D 5.
Sidalcea 'Rose Queen'. Taller at 120 cm with large rose-coloured 'Mallow' flowers. D 5.
Sidalcea 'Wm. Smith'. One of the best, with large flowers of soft salmon on 100 cm spikes. D 5.

Smilacina racemosa

A choice woodland plant akin to *Polygonatum*, the 'Solomon's Seal', with a definite preference for cool shady situations with reasonable moisture. It has 90 cm stems of arching sprays bearing creamy-white scented flowers from April to May. D 5.

Solidago 'Goldenmosa'.

Stachys lanata 'Silver Carpet'.

Solidago

The 'Golden Rods' are a common weed in the United States from where they originate, but some of the more recently introduced forms bear little resemblance to their forbears. These newer varieties are much shorter, with attractive foliage and mostly large flower heads, and of easy cultivation. Sun and good drainage is preferred but some shade tolerated.

Solidago 'Cloth of Gold'. Dwarf growing to only 45 cm, this variety has heads of deep yellow flowers in August and September. D 4.

S. 'Crown of Rays'. An unusually attractive 'Golden Rod' with deep yellow horizontal sprays on dense bushes of deep green foliage. Flowers in July and August. D 4.

S. 'Goldenmosa'. One of the most attractive and popular varieties with golden-yellow Mimosa-like flowers to 75 cm in height in August and September. D 5.

S. 'Golden Thumb'. Aptly named since it grows to only 25 cm, the miniature bushes producing fine heads of bright yellow flowers in May and June. D 6.

Stachys

Useful trouble-free plants, mostly requiring sun and reasonable drainage.

Stachys densiflorum. A little-known but attractive plant with neat mounded foliage from which is produced sturdy 45 cm spikes bearing bright pink flowers. These begin in June and bloom until August. D 5.

Stachys lanata 'Sheila MacQueen'. An improved form of this species and only recently introduced. It has large grey-green silky 'Lambs Ears' leaves and silvery flower spikes 30–45 cm high from June until August. D 4.

S. l. 'Silver Carpet'. This is one of the best low-growing ground covers in existence and more useful and attractive for the fact that it does not flower. The bright silvery-grey felty leaves make rapid growth in spring to quickly cover ground, making an ideal contrast to other foliage shrubs or Perennials. It will flourish in almost any well-drained or even dry position, sun or part shade. D 4.

Stachys macrantha 'Robusta'. A strong-growing plant making leafy clumps while sturdy 60 cm spikes bear large purple-violet flowers from May until July. There is also an attractive form with lilac-pink flowers called 'Rosea Superba'. Both D 4.

Tellima grandiflora 'Purpurea'

Included not so much as a border plant but as an excellent ground-cover subject. It grows strongly though not invasively to produce evergreen leafy clumps of bronze purple-green foliage to 30 cm and 60 cm sprays of buff flowers in late spring. Growing in sun or shade, this is an easy and attractive ground cover which should be more widely known. D 4.

Thalictrum

Includes some choice and some rather weedy species and varieties in its genus. Some of the latter grow far too tall for today's gardens and require rather a lot of maintenance. Most prefer moist fertile soils. Only a few need be mentioned below.

Thalictrum angustifolium. Grows erectly to 150 cm with almost glossy stems and leaves topped with sprays of sulphur-yellow. Flowering is in June and July. D 4–5.

Thalictrum aquilegiifolium 'Album'. Makes a magnificent display of fluffy white flower heads from May until July even if its height at 120 cm may be too much for some gardens. D 5.

T. a. 'Purpureum'. A selected form of the species with loose fluffy heads of purple-mauve from May until July. At 90 cm the height is rather more manageable. D 5.

Thalictrum dipterocarpum. Although a lovely plant with delicate foliage reminiscent of the 'Maidenhair Fern', it is rather too tall at 185 cm to consider in any but the largest garden. The many-branched stems will need supporting before the lavender, yellow centred flowers make an appearance in July lasting through until September. D 5.

Tiarella

The 'Foam Flower' is another plant preferring woodland conditions, cool, moist soil and some shade, but is also a useful ground coverer. There are several species but only two are mentioned here.

Tiarella cordifolia. Creeping habit, 25 cm spikes bearing masses of feathery white flowers in May and June. The species *collina*, though taller at 30 cm is rather more adaptable. D 5.

Tradescantia virginiana

These are invaluable Perennials of an adaptable and long-flowering nature. Growing successfully in all but very dry soils they are quite happy in full sun or some shade. All

Thalictrum aquilegiifolium *'Album'.*   Tradescantia *'Purewell Giant'.*

have ample rush-like growth and many small three-petalled flowers opening in June and lasting until September. Only a few distinct varieties can and need be mentioned.

Tradescantia 'Isis'. Deep blue flowers for a long period on 45 cm rush-like clumps D 4–5.

   T. 'Osprey'. Has snow-white flowers with a striking central tuft of blue. Height 45 cm. D 4–5.

   T. 'Purewell Giant.' The closest to red with large carmine-purple flowers. Slightly taller at 60 cm. D 4–5.

   T. 'Purple Dome'. An outstanding variety with rich velvety purple flowers. Similar height to 'Purewell Giant'. D 4–5.

Trollius

Generally regarded as moisture or waterside plants, the 'Globeflowers' will grow on any fertile garden soil which does not dry out. They are early summer-flowering subjects making compact clumps with fibrous roots and large yellow or golden buttercup-like flowers.

Trollius 'Canary Bird'. Has large lemon flowers on 75 cm stems in May and June. D 4–5.

Trollius europaeus 'Superbus'. Always makes a good show with clear light yellow flowers in May and June on 75 cm stems. D 4–5.

Trollius 'Fireglobe'. A beautiful deep orange-flowered variety. Growing to 75 cm it flowers in May and June. D 5.

Trollius 'Goldquelle'. One of the finest pure yellows, flowering in May and June. Height 75 cm. D 4–5.

Trollius ledebouri 'Golden Queen'. A distinctive taller form, the large deep orange flowers being borne on strong 90 cm stems, later than most other varieties, in June and July. D 5.

Verbascum

Showy plants although not all long lived, they provide good value where conditions suit them. Verbascums prefer a sunny but above all well-drained position. All have long fleshy roots, and while those that come from seed are short lived others which are

Trollius *'Goldquelle'.* Verbascum thapisforme (densiflorum).

A summer view across several Island Beds at Bressingham, creating a bright patchwork of contrasting form and colour.

grown from root cuttings are more reliably perennial. Even here longevity will be assisted by cutting back hard after flowering.

Verbascum 'Cotswold Queen'. Has rosettes of deep green leaves and 90 cm branched spikes carrying soft amber flowers with a purple centre. These start in June and last until August. D 5.

Verbascum 'Gainsborough' A most attractive form with soft greyish hairy leaves and handsome 90 cm spikes of pale yellow from June until August. Dislikes winter wet. D 5.

Verbascum 'Golden Bush'. This is a distinctive plant, quite different from any other *Verbascum*, with masses of twiggy 60 cm stems bearing yellow flowers from June until August. D 5.

Verbascum 'Mont Blanc'. The combination of soft, felty grey leaves and tall 120 cm spikes of pure white flowers is unusually attractive. Flowers appear in June and July. D 5.

Verbascum 'Pink Domino'. A popular variety with 100 cm spikes of deep lilac-rose flowers contrasting effectively with the dark purplish leaves. Flowers last from June until August. D 5.

Verbascum thapisforme *(densiflorum)* is one of the strongest-growing and most perennial Verbascums with deep green rosetted and erect 120 cm spikes of clustered deep yellow flowers from June until August. D 5.

Veronica

The 'Speedwells' are a large and valuable family of hardy plants, many of which are classed as alpines, and also some very good border Perennials of generally easy culture. If they have any preference it would be for sun and good drainage but many are adaptable to some shade.

Veronica gentianoides. Always makes a marvellous show in May and June with 60 cm spikes bearing many light china-blue flowers. It is an easy grower which may need dividing every three or four years, but always reliable. D 4.

 V. g. 'Variegata'. Has prettily variegated green and white leaves, somewhat less tall at 45 cm than the species, and rather deeper blue flowers appearing in May and June. D 5.

Veronica incana. A good front of the border plant with light grey foliage and contrasting deep blue flowers, on 30 cm spikes. Flowering is from June until August but not always reliable. Though it has leaves of a less distinct grey-green the variety 'Saraband', with 50 cm spikes of violet-blue, is more showy in flower. Both D 5.

Veronica longifolia 'Foerster's Blue'. A reliable perennial 'Speedwell' with dense 60 cm spikes of rich blue flowers from June until August. D 5.

Veronica teucrium. This and its varieties are some of the easiest and most attractive Perennials, making a real splash of colour in early summer. Best for a frontal position. All flower from June until August.

 V. t. 'Blue Fountain'. Makes a really dazzling picture when in full flower with myriads of gentian-blue flowers on 60 cm stems. D 5.

 V. t. 'Crater Lake Blue'. A reliable and showy form, dwarfer at 30 cm than the above, with vivid Mediterranean-blue flowers. D 5.

Veronica virginica 'Alba'. The tallest, most imposing representative of the genus, has slender erect 150 cm spikes with white flowers in August and September. D 4.

Vinca

The often despised 'Periwinkles' are not, of course, plants for perennial borders or beds but are attractive in flower and foliage and will grow and spread happily in situations

Top right: Veronica *'Foerster's Blue'.*
Bottom right: Veronica *'Blue Fountain'.*
Below: Veronica virginica *'Alba'.*

The orange flowers of Asclepias tuberosa *contrast well with imposing spikes of* Yucca filamentosa.

which are often difficult to fill. They are at home in full sun or in dry shade under trees but will take longer to establish in such situations. All are evergreen.

Vinca major. The most vigorous large-leaved 'Periwinkle' makes an excellent ground cover where little else will grow, sun or shade. Clumps 45 cm high produce masses of long leafy shoots quickly covering the ground. Large bright blue flowers are mostly seen in April and May. D 3.

    V. m. 'Variegata'. Has creamy white variegated leaves and bright blue flowers slightly earlier than the species in March and April. Strong growing though not quite so rampant as the green form. D 3–4.

Vinca minor. Has much smaller leaves than *major* and is more prostrate in habit, while stems root with ease as they cover the ground. The flowers of the species are small and light blue in April and May and not to be underrated for the pretty effect they produce. This and some of the forms are quite vigorous and should be planted where they will not become a nuisance. All grow 10–15 cm in height. D 4.

    V. m. 'Alba'. An attractive white variation. D 4.

    V. m. 'Argentea Variegata'. Has small leaves of green and creamy yellow. D 4.

    V. m. 'Atropurpurea'. Reddish-purple flowers in April and May. D 4.

    V. m. 'Bowles Variety'. More compact and less rampant than other forms and at the same time much more profuse than the species with larger azure-blue flowers. D 5.

Yucca

These semi-shrubby plants associate as well with Shrubs as with Perennials and possibly could be classed as both. In the perennial border it would be preferable to plant them in some isolation where they will make fine architectural specimens. They possess narrow sword-like leaves and imposing flowering spikes clothed with pendulous cup-shaped flowers. They are long lived where given good drainage and a warm sunny position in the garden.

Yucca filamentosa. The most often offered and reliable in flower. Once established it can be expected to throw up giant 100–120 cm spikes bearing pendulous creamy white bells each summer from July until September. D 3. There are one or two variegated forms in cultivation which are worth garden space if they can be obtained.

A favourite view of the Dell Garden at Bressingham created by Alan Bloom. The natural hollow provides a restful scene in full summer with shade and moisture beds in the foreground leading to a pool at the far end.

Cortaderia selloana 'Pumila' in full autumn glory. Spikes are much shorter than selloana.

ORNAMENTAL GRASSES

No book on Perennials, however small, would be complete without some reference to Ornamental Grasses, since their popularity has increased to a great extent in recent years. That this is due to the changing tastes from colour to form and foliage there is little doubt and of course to the popularity of plants which can be used for drying and flower arranging.

Most grasses are herbaceous in that they die back in winter but some are evergreen. The majority are easy to grow, some preferring warm dry situations, others moist. However, unless pot grown, spring planting is usually advisable. Only a few of the most distinct and reliable genera, species and varieties are mentioned below from what is a very wide selection indeed.

Avena candida. Is the easiest name for an attractive grass also known as *Helichtotrichon sempervirens*. It has narrow blue-grey evergreen leaves 30–40 cm high, above which rise graceful buff flower sprays from June into summer. D 3–4.

Bouteloua gracilis (oligostachya). With the delightful common name 'Mosquito Grass' it is an easy-growing but delicate looking plant with neat foliage and 40 cm spikes bearing brown horizontal pokers. These appear in August and are held until October. D 5.

***Carex morrowii* 'Evergold'** (Variegata Aurea). This is an outstanding plant by any standards and supersedes the species *C. morrowii* which has ineffective yellow-edged leaves. This is a mound-forming grass with bright golden-yellow and green foliage, attractive winter and summer. For a foliage plant the fact that it does not flower is an advantage. D 5.

Cortaderia selloana *(argentea)*. The 'Pampas Grass' is probably the best-known grass of all. It is not a plant for the border to mix with other Perennials but best as a specimen on its own or among shrubs. Pot-grown plants are most reliable to avoid losses in transplanting and this is best done in late spring. Plants offered raised from seed cannot always be expected to produce the large white plumes so well loved in gardens, but often turn out brownish in colour and inferior in size. Flowering late summer into autumn. Height 230–250 cm. D 1.

C. s. 'Pumila'. This more compact form is a definite improvement on the more common *C. selloana*, with large plumes rising directly above the foliage to a height of only 180 cm. The sturdy flower stems hold plumes throughout winter. D 1.

Festuca ovina glauca. A popular and useful foliage 'Fescue' for ground cover or the front of the border. Low 15 cm hummocks are an intense silver-blue in summer and winter, sun or part shade. D 5.

Hakonechloa macra 'Albo-aurea'. A choice grass, slow to establish and requiring a position which is not too dry yet well drained. It will grow happily in full sun or part shade producing each year new leaves of a beautiful golden yellow with pink, cream and green markings. 25 cm in height. D 5–6.

Lasiogrostis splendens. Also known as *Stipa splendens*, this is a clump-forming grass producing semi-erect buff-shaded plumes to 90 cm from June until September. An effective flowering species. D 4.

Luzula sylvatica 'Marginata'. A most adaptable plant growing happily in moist conditions in full sun or in the driest shade under trees, or any combination between the two. Low 30 cm clumps have green, buff-edged leaves and greenish flowers in spring on 45 cm stems. D 5.

Miscanthus sacchariflorus. An ideal subject for a quick-growing screen or a hedge, this tough and hardy plant will adapt to dry or moist conditions. Spreading, though not invasive, roots act as a base for the enormous 250–300 cm green leafy canes to rise in one season from ground level. The first year after planting half this height can be expected. Foliage remains when the sap retreats in autumn and provides some windbreak for much of the winter. Flowers are seldom and indistinct. D 3.

M. sinensis 'Variegatus'. This distinctive grass provides bright foliage from spring until autumn with 120 cm stems of creamy yellow and green leaves. Grows easily in any normal soils and is particularly effective as a waterside plant. D 4.

M. s. 'Zebrinus'. A striking foliage grass with red-green leaves and horizontal golden yellow stripes. 120 cm. D 4.

Molinia coerulea 'Variegata'. A neat and showy grass with bright green and variegated leaves to 45 cm. Buff panicles of flowers rise to 60 cm, creating a hazy effect from August until October. A first-class trouble-free subject for good soil. D 5.

Stipa gigantea. Is again more of a specimen plant for use among shrubs rather than for the perennial border. It forms large leafy clumps with imposing 100 cm spikes bearing showers of golden oat-like yellow plumes in August and September. D 3–4.

List of Hardy Perennials for Special Purposes

These lists are to be used as a guide only. Some plants are able to adapt to almost a complete range of conditions from hot dry soils to shade and moisture; others are much less adaptable.

Therefore because a perennial is listed below as a plant suitable for moisture it does not necessarily mean that it cannot grow in any reasonable soil without any special moist conditions, i.e. Lythrums and many more. Please refer to the alphabetical descriptive list for more detailed information.

PLANTS SUITABLE FOR GROUND COVER

Alchemilla mollis
Armeria maritima 'Alba' 'Dusseldorf Pride'
Bergenia in variety
Campanula poscharskyana 'Stella'
Epimedium in variety
Geranium in variety
Lamium in variety
Liriope muscari
Nepeta faassenii
Pachysandra terminalis
Polygonum affine in variety
Prunella in variety
Pulmonaria in variety
Stachys lanata in variety
Tellima grandiflora 'Purpurea'
Tiarella cordifolia
Vinca in variety

ORNAMENTAL GRASSES

Carex morrowii 'Evergold'
Festuca ovina 'Glauca'
Luzula sylvatica 'Marginata'

PLANTS SUITABLE FOR MOISTURE AND WATERSIDE

Aruncus sylvester
Astilbe in variety
Astrantia in variety
Caltha palustris 'Plena'
Cimicifuga in variety
Dicentra in variety
Hemerocallis in variety
Hosta in variety
Iris sibirica in variety
Ligularia in variety
Lysimachia in variety
Polygonum bistorta 'Superbum' *milettii*
Primula denticulata rosea 'Delight'
Ranunculus in variety
Rodgersia in variety
Tradescantia in variety
Trollius in variety

ORNAMENTAL GRASSES

Miscanthus sacchariflorus sinensis 'Variegatus'

PLANTS WHICH ASSOCIATE WELL WITH SHRUBS

Acanthus spinosus
Agapanthus in variety
Alchemilla mollis
Bergenia in variety
Crocosmia in variety
Epimedium in variety
Geranium in variety
Helleborus in variety
Hemerocallis in variety
Heuchera in variety
Hosta in variety
Kniphofia in variety
Nerine bowdenii
Pachysandra terminalis
Paeonia in variety

Pulmonaria in variety
Stachys lanata in variety
Tiarella cordifolia
Vinca in variety
Yucca filamentosa

ORNAMENTAL GRASSES
Avena candida
Cortaderia selloana (argentea)
Lasiogrostis splendens
Stipa gigantea

PLANTS WITH SILVER OR GREY FOLIAGE

Achillea 'Moonshine'
Anaphalis in variety
Artemisia in variety
Dianthus in variety
Euphorbia myrsinites
Helichrysum hybridum 'Sulphur Light'
Nepeta faassenii
Stachys lanata in variety
Verbascum 'Gainsborough'
Veronica incana
Yucca filamentosa

ORNAMENTAL GRASSES
Avena candida
Festuca ovina 'Glauca'

PLANTS SUITABLE FOR HOT DRY SITUATIONS

Acanthus spinosus
Armeria 'Bees Ruby'
Catananche caerulea
Dianthus in variety
Dictamnus in variety
Eryngium in variety
Euphorbia myrsinites
Gaillardia in variety
Geranium 'Russell Prichard'
Gypsophila paniculata in variety
Kniphofia in variety
Oenothera missouriensis
Papaver orientalis in variety
Stachys lanata in variety

ORNAMENTAL GRASS
Cortaderia selloana in variety.

PLANTS SUITABLE FOR SHADE OR SEMI-SHADE

Acanthus spinosus
Aconitum in variety
Alchemilla mollis
Anaphalis in variety
Anemone japonica in variety
Aquilegia in variety
Bergenia in variety
Campanula in variety

Cimicifuga in variety
Dicentra in variety
Doronicum in variety
Epimedium in variety
Geranium endressii 'Wargrave Pink'
   'Johnson's Blue'
Helleborus corsicus
   orientalis Hybrids
   niger
Hemerocallis in variety
Heuchera in variety
Heucherella 'Bridget Bloom'
Hosta in variety
Iris pallida 'Aurea Variegata'
   'Variegata'
   sibirica in variety
   stylosa
Lamium in variety
Ligularia in variety
Liriope muscari
Lysimachia in variety
Lythrum in variety
Meconopsis betonicifolia
Monarda in variety
Nerine bowdenii
Omphalodes cappadocica 'Anthea Bloom'
Pachysandra terminalis
Phlox paniculata in variety
Physalis franchettii
Physostegia in variety
Platycodon grandiflorum in variety
Polemonium in variety
Polygonum in variety
Primula sieboldii in variety
   vulgaris
Prunella in variety
Pulmonaria in variety
Ranunculus in variety
Rodgersia in variety
Schizostylis coccinea in variety
Sidalcea in variety
Smilacina racemosa
Solidago in variety
Stachys lanata in variety
Tellima grandiflora 'Purpurea'
Thalictrum in variety
Tiarella cordifolia
Tradescantia in variety
Trollius in variety

PLANTS WHICH WILL TOLERATE DRY SHADE

Lamium galeobdolen 'Variegatum'
   maculatum Chequers
Pachysandra terminalis
Polygonum affine 'Darjeeling Red'
Tellima grandiflora 'Purpurea'
Vinca in variety

ORNAMENTAL GRASS
Luzula sylvatica 'Marginata'

Common Names

Most perennials have a common or English name, many have more than one and, of course, each country will have its own common names too. This is why the Latin or botanical name is used for national and international recognition – difficult though they can be to pronounce. Below are listed some of the English common names with their botanical or Latin equivalents alongside printed in blue.

African Lily *Agapanthus*
Alum Root *Heuchera*
Alum Root, False *Tellima grandiflora*
Avens *Geum*
Barrenwort *Epimedium*
Bear's Breeches *Acanthus*
Bee Balm *Monarda didyma*
Bell-flower *Campanula*
Bergamot *Monarda*
Bethlehem Sage *Pulmonaria saccharata*
Bishop's Hat *Epimedium*
Bistort, Common *Polygonum bistorta*
Black-eyed Susan *Rudbeckia fulgida speciosa*
Bleeding Heart *Dicentra spectabilis*
Blue Fescue *Festuca glauca*
Bugbane *Cimicifuga*
Burning Bush *Dictamnus albus*
Buttercup *Ranunculus*
Cape-gooseberry *Physalis*
Carnation *Dianthus*
Cat-mint *Nepeta*
Chinese Bell-flower *Platycodon*
Chinese Lantern *Physalis*
Christmas Rose *Helleborus niger*
Cinquefoil *Potentilla*
Columbine *Aquilegia*
Cone Flower *Rudbeckia*
Cornflower *Centaurea*
Crane's-bill *Geranium*
Day Lily *Hemerocallis*
Dead Nettle *Lamium*
Dutchman's Breeches *Dicentra*
Evening Primrose *Oenothera*
Everlasting flower *Anaphalis*
Fleabane *Erigeron*
Foam Flower *Tiarella*
Globeflower *Trollius*
Globe Thistle *Echinops*
Goldenrod *Solidago*
Greek Mallow *Sidalcea*
Jacob's-ladder *Polemonium caeruleum*
Japanese Bell-flower *Platycodon*

Kaffir Lily *Schizostylis*
Kansas Gay Feather *Liatris*
Knapweed *Centaurea*
Lady's-mantle *Alchemilla*
Lamb's Tongue *Stachys lanata*
Lenten Rose *Helleborus orientalis*
Leopard's-bane *Doronicum*
Loosestrife *Lysimachia*
Loosestrife, Purple *Lythrum*
Lungwort *Pulmonaria*
Mallow, Greek *Sidalcea*
Masterwort *Astrantia*
Meadow-rue *Thalictrum*
Meadowsweet *Filipendula ulmaria*
Michaelmas-daisy *Aster novi-belgii*
Monk's-hood *Aconitum*
Mullein *Verbascum*
Obedient Plant *Physostegia virginiana*
Oswego Tea *Monarda didyma*
Paeony *Paeonia*
Periwinkle *Vinca*
Pincushion Flower *Scabiosa*
Pink *Dianthus*
Plantain Lily *Hosta*
Poppy, Oriental *Papaver orientalis*
Red Hot Poker *Kniphofia*
Sea-pink *Armeria maritima*
Sea-lavender *Limonium*
Sedge *Carex*
Shasta Daisy *Chrysanthemum maximum*
Solomon's-seal *Polygonatum*
Sow's Ear *Stachys lanata*
Speedwell *Veronica*
Spiderwort *Tradescantia*
Spurge *Euphorbia*
Sunflower, Orange *Heliopsis*
Sunflower, Perennial *Helianthus*
Thrift *Armeria maritima*
Torch Lily *Kniphofia*
Wood Rush *Luzula*
Woundwort *Stachys*
Yarrow *Achillea millefolium*